No Half Measures

Marilyn Lamont

ISBN: 978-1-905451-78-4

A CIP catalogue for this book is available from the National Library.

This book was published in cooperation with
Choice Publishing & Book Services Ltd, Ireland
Tel: 041 9841551 Email: info@choicepublishing.ie
www.choicepublishing.ie

Acknowledgements

I dedicate this book to the following members of my family, for without whom; there would be no book to write.

I truly thank my beloved husband Tom, for having the love and faith in me to recover.
My grandmother Mary and my grandfather Duncan, may they both rest in peace.
My mother Patricia, R.I.P., my brother wee Jim, my aunt Cathie and uncle John. Also my uncle Duncan and aunt Bridget, R.I.P.
My true friends and the fellowship of AA and finally God, for carrying me through from the Gates of Hell to Heaven on Earth.

Since going to print, sadly my beloved father (Bertie) has died. I thank him for the eighteen wonderful sober years we had together. May he Rest in Peace.

Many thanks to the following contributors to the book:
Artwork and cover: Tom McKimm
Editing: "Christine" at Flytte
Publishing: Choice Publishing and Book Services Ltd,

Part One
My Old Life

"You should write a book, about your life Marilyn." If I had a penny for every time people said this to me, I would be a very rich lady for sure and I was still, after all, only in my twenties. "What life?" you may say. Too young perhaps, to have any story to tell. Not so, in fact, I could have easily filled a book with enough life story then, to make "War and Peace" seem like a pocket book.

But no, I was not only still too young, but too busy having a 'Good Time' partying too busy drinking, too busy being an alcoholic. Today I am fifty, more than twice the age I was back then and today people still say "You should write a book about your life Marilyn." Today I feel, the time is now right, for today I feel I have actually lived two lives in one lifetime. Because today, I am sober. My old life ended on a very dark day, in 1985, when I was suicidal, drunk, and beat by booze, and my new life began that same day in 1985 when I got sober. Not wishing to mix my reader up any further, I shall "Start at the Start" as my mother would say.

I was born in 1954 in then, quite a busy industrial town, in the west of Scotland 'on the Clyde' named Greenock. A lovely bright magical house in the very centre of town. A happy house filled with music, laughter and love, love from my wonderful Granny and devoted grandfather, whom I called Mum and Dad. Although my Granny was a strict, very religious Victorian woman, I loved her with a passion as after all, she raised me from birth. 'Drinks a Curse' she would squeal, 'only a curse.' My Granny was a strict Catholic and therefore a Pioneer of sobriety also.

My Granny after all, was born in 1899, lived through two world wars, saw horror and hardship, saw also for many generations, what damage and carnage drink did to people and families alike. But before you sigh, dear reader, I am not a preacher I will only tell you my life as it was, and as it now is, and I only hope that throughout these pages, if you will only bear with me, hopefully, you will laugh, perhaps cry, but most of all, come to believe that no matter how great your own struggle can be through life, that there is hope, and no such thing as a "hopeless case."

I could say that I am living proof of that. My mother met my father in 1952 while she at that time was a very well known accordionist, and toured with many great dance bands of the fifties. The Great Jimmy Shand Band, Andy Stewart and the White Heather Club etc, being very popular throughout Scotland. But alas, she was to meet my father at the Parochial Hall Dance in a small town named Moville in County Donegal, where we lived for five full months of the summer season while my mother toured and played in halls, throughout Ireland working with many great Irish dance bands and musicians. I chuckle though, when I recall her telling me of how she first met my father as she played in the band that night at the Parochial Hall. He staggered drunk around the floor, swinging, swaying and trying to dance, catching her eye on his journey past the stage. Handsome in a rugged way, tall with a shock of blue-black hair, still, did not change the fact that he was drunk. And with being tea total herself, there was no way she was going to be lumbered with him and don't forget, she also had my Granny to face who would certainly be waiting up for her to return home from the dance. No, the torture of a drunkard was the last thing she needed. So she left the dancehall alone. Although being extremely beautiful and glamorous, tall, platinum blonde, expertly made-up from head to toe, my mother was a stunning woman but humble natured enough with a beautiful personality to match her looks. She was may I add, so very down to earth in attitude and did not ever realise the total impact these had on meeting people. They really did adore her and my father then pursued her continually until she gave in and agreed to go out with him eventually. He wooed her with his charm on a continual basis day and night with money, fast cars and just constant persistent persuasion.

When, in the end, even my strict Granny accepted him and six months later on Boxing Day 1952 my mother and father married.

Although my father came from the town of Strabane in Northern Ireland, he and my mother decided to marry in her home town of Greenock. It amazes me to this day how I got to be here at all for my mother herself told me that even on their honeymoon night, my father spent it in the hotel bar the whole night long drinking as resident, well into the next morning. However, on June 9th 1954 I appeared and shortly after that my father disappeared and I was left with my granny.

My mother left home to work to keep me basically and I seldom saw her. She was more like a distant sister to me in my childhood. I would call her by her first name Patricia, and not mother. In my eyes my granny was my mother and my father was my grandfather. The two people who were always there for me. My mother became legally separated from my father when I was five years old and I distinctly remember that being the last I saw of him. I would not have his name mentioned to me. I would cry, stamp and scream "He's not my father," and I had a horrific fear of drunken men. A phobia in fact that I would not even pass a drunkard in the street, for fear it might be my father. My Granny was right, drink was a curse.

My grandfather although also an excellent musician, worked hard all his life in the torpedo factory in Alexandria near Clydebank, and would start his day at dawn travelling on the old ferry over the Clyde every day while at weekends he would also play in the dance bands locally. A fine gentle man with a wonderful quiet gentle nature to match and I distinctly remember him to this day, smiling, playing his accordion and as my mother also ran a dancing school for Highland, Irish, Tap Dancing etc. I too, was put on stage from three years old. Although I never could dance (my mother would joke I had wooden feet) I loved to sing and I was sent to piano lessons from age five. Religiously every Sunday I would trudge to my Piano teacher Mr. Sanderson and sit and play wee easy songs from his music sheet, but then I'd go home, and play my own by ear. Not music. I much preferred playing "my own way" as I called it and sing, sing, sing, that's all I wanted to do. I remember the evening so well, when my beloved Grandfather wound up his alarm clock literally for the last time. It was to be the first truly sad blow to my young life. On retiring the following day from the torpedo factory, he was to receive his gold watch on his final day at work. "This'll be the last time I'll have to wind the old clock Mary", he said to my Granny "I can sit up all hours after tomorrow I won't be thinking about work."

I remember at seven years old coming home from school the following day to horrific sadness, and confusion. I was sent upstairs to a neighbour while my Granny had to try to make her way to the Vale of Leven Hospital in Alexandria, as my grandfather had taken a cerebral haemorrhage at his retirement function, and had died.

It was such a shock to the family that little did we know that it was his last day. I felt orphaned again and I was left with my Granny. My mother gave up the School of Dancing and now toured constantly with her band working for long periods of time as a resident red coat at Butlins Holiday Camp. She would send me regular letters, pocket money etc. money to my Granny to keep us. Although now without my Grandfathers wage, we spent many years with my Granny making do, mending my clothes, buying me coats for school "to grow into" three sizes too big. I remember always having clothes "to grow into". By the time I grew into one lot, it was time "to grow into" another outfit. However, in spite of just me and "Mum" (Granny) I was happy enough. She would attend parent's nights at school. She was always there I loved her dearly and would defend her when cruel school kids would tease "Is that old lady your Mum?" I would flare up instantly, never afraid of anyone or anybody. I had the head of an old person on my shoulders. I was with my Granny constantly everywhere together. I played and sang twice a week for the local pensioners functions my Granny belonged to. All her friends where pensioners and I loved that. Strict and all as my Granny was, I could get around her my own way. I was seldom at school either. Always sick, my Granny said I was "towty" and old Scottish word meaning vulnerable to illness. I wasn't only "towty" I was fly. "Sleikit" an old Scottish word meaning cunning and sly, and I loved that.

Although by now my mother had stopped travelling back and forward to Donegal my Granny and I, continued as usual for four months of the summer season every year without fail. We loved going to Ireland. We would chat all winter long about "Ireland", "About Moville" happy days. My Granny was large to say the least "as broad as she was long" she'd say. Sixteen stone and God fearing my Granny was nobody's fool and would "swing for me" many times. I feared her as much as I loved her. The only person I loved so much I also feared so much. But I had to remember she was mother, father, everything to me and that could not have been easy for her either. And she ruled with an iron rod. I have an Aunt Cathie, who lived with us, my Granny also reared her. I call Cathie my Aunt, but actually my Granny was her blood Aunt, and took her in at a very young age from her sister whom due to ill health felt Cathie was happier with my Granny. And Cathie was happy with us, only as a child, I could not see eye to eye with Cathie. She was twenty seven years old when I was born. She was clever and wise, and most of all she could see through my flyness, and knew all my "sleikit" ways. I did not like that one bit, and would taunt and torture her knowing my Granny would take my part. "Don't even your wit to a wean" my Granny would shout at Cathie when we argued. But I would instigate the row I would cause the argument. I was full of devilment, and my Aunt Cathie suffered.

I was always an odd child. I always felt different with my old head on my shoulders. I had no school friends as such and would entertain myself. I was obsessive about things. I was obsessed with shopwork and would take my pocket money every week and buy paper bags in bulk and for Christmas I always got every year a toy cash register. When other children were getting dolls, prams, etc, I was getting sellotape machines, office equipment, shop display boxes, and little money making stunts like my chocolate machine. Knowing full well my Granny had a weakness for the tasty small penny bars of chocolate from my machine, I'd charge her two pence and quickly discovered my profits early.

I laugh now when I recall my Granny rising in the morning looking for her teeth and I would have them plucked from the tumbler of Sterodent, and wrapped in a bag with a price on it. "This shop over here sells teeth at a shilling" or as she'd stumble round looking for her glasses I'd cry "Glasses at three pence" and newspapers etc knowing full well my Granny would eventually good naturally "buy" back her belongings. She got really so very angry though when one Sunday morning she searched and searched for her "stays" corsets that is. Whilst I promptly produced them ready wrapped at half a crown. I got some clout that day not only for my cheek, but I also made her late for Mass into the bargain.

With no such thing as income support back then, times were tight for a pensioner to bring up a child and although my mother sent funds to help us, for the first time in my Granny's life, and at an age when people retired, she had to now at sixty five, go out and try to find a job.

She applied for many posts, but without any success and although fit, well and capable, her age was still very much against her. That is, until one day whilst searching the local "Telegraph" she came upon an advert, whereby a young man was seeking an experienced preferably elder lady to look after, and basically child mind his two young children whilst he returned to the army.

My Granny applied immediately and very soon found herself summoned to an interview, not from the children's father, but from their own Gran Rose.

Gran Rose was very bossy and may I add rather snobby, and just did not have the time or patience to child mind her own grandchildren of whom there were two, a girl of three years old, and a boy of two. Sadly, the children had been dumped in the local corner café by their mother whom absconded with an American sailor from the Holy Loch Army based at Dunoon. And horrifically on telling the café owner she would be back soon, she had no intention of returning and never did. So, as their own father was away in the army his mother, Gran Rose, had sole charge of the children, that is until my Granny appeared for the interview and got the job.

My Granny was delighted with her new post and although the wage then was poor enough five pounds a week, my Granny would journey every morning by bus and collect the two children from Gran Rose to mind for the day.

The children were truly beautiful in looks. Lyn was a very pretty child with fair hair and eyes like large round saucers, and Alan was blonde, chubby and a typical little boy. But both still a handful for a women of my Granny's age to mind; and for two years, my Granny took orders and commands from Gran Rose on a daily basis until one day, when my mother returned on a short visit home, realised that my Granny was being used and dictated to by this obnoxious woman, whom, my mother felt should have been minding her own grand children. My mother on seeing my Granny in tears, promptly telephoned Gran Rose with a sharp piece of her mind, telling her to "Do the job herself." The children had grown to love my Granny and she likewise, they even called her "Granny" and would cry when she had to leave them each day. So it was very hard for my Granny to severe the bond she had with Lyn and Alan, but on leave from the army, their father and Gran Rose called to our house and apologised to my Granny for the ill treatment and on seeing the children suffer, my Granny returned to her job – on her terms. The children moved in with us now completely and became a big part of our life and for twelve years through good and bad times, my Granny had now another two children raised.

One day out of the blue, twelve years later Lyn and Alan's father announced he was about to remarry, and requested the children whom were teenagers now, return to him and his new wife. My Granny was very sad and hurt to see the children go but their new life lay ahead, and although the children did not wish to leave my Granny, especially Alan whom was so very close to us, and still is today, they had little option but to go with their father and their new stepmother. It never did work and most days the children would call home to us from school and to not wish to go back to their new home. This went on for years until both children (now adults) went in search of their own mother in America, with Alan always keeping in touch with us to this very day.

In 1963 my mother had met a new man in her life and not a very choice character may I add, and rather too fond of the drink. My Granny totally despised him on introduction and forbade my mother instantly from seeing this man. For a beautiful woman like my mother who didn't drink, she had this strange ability to choose alcoholics and total losers as partners. "Why did she choose these "eegits?" I would question but that was my mothers business, even although she, I felt, should have, for once this time, taken my Granny's advice. But no, she chose Jim or "Jaws" as I grew to name him. For to me, he looked like a fish, and drank like one. I also never could take to "Jaws." I felt he had no time for me anyhow, and would say, "I'll fix you lady when you come to stay with me and your mother" and my Granny would fix him, by severally letting him know, it would be "Over her dead body."

The clanger came totally when at forty two years old, my mother produced a child, a boy she named Jim. Before this, she tried in vain to hide "the pregnancy" from my Granny going as far as choosing to have Wee Jim adopted out. My mother's brother Duncan and his wife Bridget agreed to adopt Jim as one of their own, and take him to live with them at their home in London, where he would have everything money could buy. My Uncle Duncan is a very well known Jazz musician, and Wee Jim would have had a very comfortable upbringing with Duncan's own two boys. But alas, my mother changed her mind at the last minute, and decided to keep Wee Jim. My Granny outraged and angry feeling disgraced, brought on by my mother to the family, actually totally banished my mother and Wee Jim not only from the house, from the town itself. Sending them to England with my mother's shame and disgrace she left my life once more with her new child, and once more I was left with my Granny.

Two years passed and still my Granny would not relent or accept my mother or Wee Jim. She could not even bring herself to mention their names. Don't forget, my Granny was "old school" and a child out of wedlock was a condemnation on the family, especially a good living Catholic family and my Granny stuck firmly to her decision to disown them both. That is, until Father Moloney gave her a telling off for being unchristian towards her own and told her "She was sinning more than my mother had." All my mother had done was to have a little baby but Father Maloney did the trick by pointing this out to my Granny and if Father Moloney told her off she'd listen. So my mother and Wee Jim were accepted into our lives and immediately, returned from London. My mother left Wee Jim with my Granny whilst she went off with "Jaws" to look for accommodation. Surely my Granny would not have yet another child to raise?

Wee Jim was an adorable child even with his English accent and cute looks it still took my Granny time to fully accept him but she did and loved him like her own. Very soon he acquired the Scottish twang and was coming to Ireland every summer with now Lyn, Alan, Wee Jim, and me. My Granny had her hands truly full.

Moville was my saving grace, I loved the holiday time there. I would have four months of the year free from school which I truly hated. I was seldom at school, if I could have left school at ten years old I would have ran. I truly don't know how I have any degree of education at all today. My Granny did send me for some private tuition to her old teacher friend, Mrs O'Connor, but my heart was never in education only music. My private tuition with Mrs. O'Connor was short lived. I still was average and failed my eleven plus, but all I was interested in was the fact that I could rattle any song off, on my big old piano, and sing my heart out to suit myself.

I only ever had one friend in childhood whom I worshiped. Her name was also Patricia. I met Patricia in primary school, and our friendship was second to none. I didn't mind failing my eleven plus one bit, because Patricia also failed hers so we were certainly going "down" together to the Loreto Girls School in Greenock. No high grade passes for us, no St. Columba's High School, no we were "failures." We were Loreto Girls, and we were delighted.

Where you saw Patricia, you saw me too "Inseparable," "Joined at the hip," my Granny would say. We joined girl guides together and I will never forget my first dance, a Boy Scout dance in Saint Patrick's Hall. God, I felt ugly. My Granny had dressed me in a flowerily frock and ankle socks with ringlets in my hair, and I was thirteen. I was such a wallflower not one dance did I get. Nobody, not even the ugliest Boy Scout came near me. I swore that night as I cried myself to sleep I would never ever be a wallflower again.

I had inherited my Granny's high cheek colouring and although beautiful on my Granny, I hated it. I would devise ways of bleaching my skin to remove my red cheeks and don't know to this day how I have any decent skin on my face, for I used every household item to remove my high colour, which of course I never could. My buck teeth didn't help. I would look at myself in the mirror with my big red face, and puppy fat and cry. I needed to change and change drastically and my appetite was huge. I could eat two school dinners a day and with my Granny's best friend as dinner lady, this I often did. No, I was fat and ugly and I had to change now.

Anorexia Nervosa was practically unheard of when I was thirteen, I certainly hadn't a clue it existed. But in my mind, what I thought was a very logical mind, I decided to slim. I tried and tried without success until one day I said to Patricia "It's the food, if I don't eat the food, I would not get fat." It was so simple. Stop eating. I had to stop eating completely to loose weight and that's just what I did. I totally stopped eating immediately. I made Patricia promise that if she saw me eat she would take my portions or any food from me. It was hard at first. The hunger pains were sore, and my willpower had to be strong. Fasting became easy. When I saw my new slim figure emerge I was delighted and all thoughts of food would vanish from my mind. In fact the thought of eating petrified me. My Granny was demented with worry, she had me visit four separate doctors about my weight loss, which was drastic. My Granny would buy best steak chops, chicken etc all expensive foods, she could ill afford and I'd destroy it immediately. Fly, by God I was fly. My devious nature flourished in anorexia, hiding food, feeding it to the dog, scooping the egg out of the boiled egg shell before my

Granny could blink. Making a fake bisto gravy on an empty plate with illusion I'd eaten steak. Not a bite not a crumb would pass my lips. I lived on coffee and chewing gum and didn't know I was on a slow suicide slope. One evening whilst I sat rolled in a cushion, at weighting six stone, my Aunt Cathie began to cry and pointed out to my poor Granny, that I was dying. I had little hair left on my head. My bones were sticking through my flesh and even my buck teeth were sitting out on my chin. I was sick, very sick. I had been sent home from school with a note for my Granny saying "Was I in bad health?" I was fainting everywhere and I was being constantly taken by ambulance to hospital, whereby the minute I would come round and see food I would promptly discharge myself.

I had made myself a large long corset. I had gathered over a dozen of Wee Jim and Alan's elastic school snake belts. I carefully sewed them altogether making one long garment I could tighten to suit me. My gruesome corset started below my arms, covered my chest, and reached well below my buttocks. It was like a huge item of elastic torture, but I would not leave the house without my great invention tightened right around my whole body which by now was basic skin and bone. My Granny knew nothing of the corset until she once more, dragged me to the doctors whereby, I fainted in his very surgery with the startled Doctor discovering my corset. He had immediately cut it off me it was so tight to remove with scissors. My Granny was crying and begging the doctor to help. The doctor to my delight said "She must be eating, she'll be eating in cafes." This suited me fine. He really did not have a clue about my severe anorexia and that suited me. Although now, Wee Jim and Alan had an explanation for their many missing snake belts.

Makeup was my God. I'd plaster my frail face with thick pan stick, black eyeliner, deep red lips, and I hid behind my mask, with my Granny so strict against "face paint" as she called it.

She would discover my precious makeup and continually burn it giving me a hiding also. I'd be sent from every classroom to "wash my face." I was a complete rebel, hated authority. I had sworn I would change and by God I had certainly changed. I felt I had my anorexia controlled as I now made my coffee more milky. "That's fine" Doctor Travers said to my Granny, "Sure babies live solely on milk." I stopped weighing myself every day. I seemed to maintain a stick like appearance which was so very fashionable in the late sixties. Although my friend Patricia and my small dog continued to "Eat for Two." They both were expanding whilst I made Twiggy look like "Fat Nan The Boxer."

My poor Granny now in her seventies would trudge daily to the co-op heaving home pints of milk to keep me alive. It was sad, and I should never have allowed her to carry these huge weights.

Daily my whole personality changed. I still sang at the pensioners concerts but now I had this compelling feeling that I was too young to be mixing with the old folk. I began to get crabbit with my beloved Granny. I slept with my Granny all my life and now couldn't bear to be in the same room with her. I was obsessive. I had one large coffee cup and I would never ever allow it to be washed. I'd scream at my Granny if she attempted to wash my cup. I was paranoid now, seeing a psychiatrist and don't forget that all of this, was even before I had lifted a drink.

My mother, who was now living in Paisley with Wee Jim and Jaws, was summoned home by my Granny to see if she hopefully could help me, but I had become so very obnoxious even with my mild mannered mother, and with her seeing the shape I had become she started to cry, with then my Granny crying "She hates me Tricia, she hates me." I didn't hate my beloved Granny, I was just sick. I told my Granny that "I needed my own room". I felt I was being constantly spied on, but there was no other bedroom free. Aunt Cathie had her own room with a lock and key as well. It was just so damned unfair, in my opinion. I would hide unwanted food in a locker I had obtained, but I would forget about if for weeks and the stench would be overpowering with my Granny dragging beds and furniture about looking for dead rats it was so bad. I would remember my forgotten unwanted meat and I'd unlock my locker to face the horror within. My Granny's strong faith in her religion annoyed me. I stopped going to Mass, stopped singing for Fathers Molonies Pensioners. I removed all my Granny's holy pictures from our bedroom, and replaced them with Mick Jagger, Black Sabbath, and a host of other unpleasant faces that would have frightened ghosts.

My Granny was furious, she would rip the posters from the wall. I would just replace them. My Aunt Cathie had told her that she saw me in Woolworths, my face caked in make-up, false eyelashes etc. My Granny would hammer me, burn the make-up, always threatening me with "I'll get the Priest to deal with you." It got so awful and I still had the horrific fear of my Granny for at her age, she was still well able to "swing for me." It even got to the stage that she would make me describe the actual colour of the Priests garments on a Sunday, and she would question me on the gospel read that day. I had to prove my every move. I now stopped going to music lessons with Mr. Sanderson. I would sit in the cafe instead. This happened too regularly, until Mr. Sanderson phoned my Granny looking for me and "Why I was not attending my music", me ending up with another chastising, and I can assure you, my Granny would not "miss me and hit the wall." She meant business.

I had a boyfriend in secret of course, a milk delivery boy two years older than me, two feet smaller than me, and two weeks later his wee mother was at my Granny's door telling her to "Keep me away from her boy." Yes, another hiding. My Granny said "I was a disgrace." She did not get the Priest to me as promised, instead she got my mother to call back down from Paisley to see to me. My mother was so easy going in comparison to my Granny, and my mother said "Marilyn, if you just wait until you are fifteen and left school, then you can do the things you want to do, like wearing make-up, mini-skirts etc, please just wait until you leave school for my sake." But that was six months away. How could I face the world without my camouflage until then? I justified it by saying to myself, "I'll calm the makeup down a bit, less paint, one coat of emulsion instead of three. Yes, that's what I'd do, I'd go "natural." That idea lasted all of half a minute. No, there was absolutely no half measures for me.

At fourteen, my fifteenth birthday seemed a lifetime away. It's so strange how when young we have the desire to be older, and when older, we often have the desire to be young. Was I ever happy? And rather than calm my face paint down, as I had promised, I proceeded to pile on the war paint to the "Full Monty." Living with Granny in a tenement building, I would religiously leave the house daily with my "Rosy" clean face and slap on my face paint in the close only to scrub it clean before returning home to face my usual ritual of my Granny's inspections and holy holy lifestyle. Whereby, the only thing I was religious with then, where my obsessions. My obsession to be thinner, fat terrified me rigid. Granny was fat, and I could never and would never allow that to happen to me. I would die first. My obsession with my looks, I detested my red face and my fathers buck teeth, I knew I had inherited from him. My obsession with my mothers good looks. How could I not have inherited those? Her beautiful looks so glamorous, expertly made up, never a platinum blonde hair out of place. Her wonderful personality and good nature, her genius ability to play her music to perfection. While me, I was "Mrs. No Hope", with my Granny's fat body, red face, and my fathers buck teeth and just average at playing my music. No, being fourteen was sore, I had a big act to follow in my mother, and I swore I would do just that.

Across the road from my all girls Loreto school, was a garage repair shop. Whereby I noticed a very handsome young man, whom may I add, half the school population had also noticed and a much older fellow whom I took to be the boss.

Wolf whistles would bombard me daily from the garage as I pranced to school, done up like a dish of fish. Skirt hoisted around my waist to pelmet size, strutting out like Miss World. Yes, the young fellow fancied me and I was ecstatic when one day he waved me over for a chat, perhaps a date? But my desires were short lived when I go there only to discover to my absolute horror it was the old boy who fancied me, leered after me, wolf whistled and wanted a date.

Oh no, I cried to the young boy, I now knew as Tommy, as he put me wise to old "Quins" philandering ways. "He's married," Tommy put me right, "Don't say I told you, or I'll lose my job." I didn't need Tommy to put me wise, Quin wasn't just only married, he was ancient old, at least forty and ugly, where as Tommy, now, he was a different kettle of fish. He would do me nicely. Tommy was two years older than me, tall, dark and handsome. Just the job, with a lovely quiet personality to match his good looks. Yes, he would do me nicely, as we secretly dated on a daily basis. The envy of my girl school, I was elated, only now, was I not only hiding my unwanted food, face paint, and short skirts from my Granny, now I was also hiding Tommy.

We sneaked our meetings meticulously around my Granny's whereabouts, going to cafes, going for walks, I recall mentioning my mother to Tommy and we made great plans to visit her. One Sunday morning instead of going to Mass we decided to go to Paisley to visit my mother. We boarded the train at Greenock and as we drew into Paisley train station I felt shocked, stupid and embarrassed only to find, I did not knew where my mother lived.

I never ever was allowed to visit my mother, as she now lived with "Jaws." I never before had any great desire to visit. She had her own life, always did, so how would I know her address. Unbelievable as it sounds, it's so true. My mother only a thirty minute train journey from my home and I didn't know her address. As we sat in a local park bench I embarrassingly muttered something to Tommy about 'Forgetting my notes of my mothers address' and Tommy just smiled, took me for a coffee and headed back home to Greenock on the next train.

We arrived back in Greenock still early enough for me to know my Granny was out at Mass and usually once the Mass ended she would take tea in the Chapel Hall, meeting up with her old cronies and pals. So what better time for me to smuggle Tommy into the house; even for an hour or so, and perhaps a coffee, and listen to my latest records. For after all, I had already took him miles to Paisley on a fools errand, surely it was the least I could do? Or so I thought. We had only just finished our coffee, and just as I placed my pile of records on my old dansette record player, suddenly the door burst open, in barged my Granny, like a fiend, grabbed poor Tommy by the shoulders and physically threw him out on to the landing and down every stair in the close barging back into the house to deal with me. "Hussy" she squealed thrashing out at me, "Wash that face, before I label it unrecognisable" skelping me about the head in the process, she would as she called it herself "draw off." And just hit whatever part of my person that came in contact with her aim and that usually was my face and head. But I loved my Granny and I knew not to defy her ever. But sure with me; there were no half measures.

Eventually, my fifteenth birthday arrived at last. Even my mother visited us that day for a bit of support for me, for this was D-day. The great unveiling of my painted face. Everything I possessed in my make-up bag got plastered slapped and trowelled onto to my face, with not one, but two sets of false eyelashes as well. If I was going to get the go-ahead from my Granny she was as well to see the full works.

"Oh Mother of God Tricia" she screamed at my mother "She's like a coo looking o'er a dyke, with they coal black eyes, and rid lips." She squealed at my mother in her broad Scots accent translated reader, this means roughly, "A cow looking over a wall, Oh my God a Jezebel, What will the neighbours says?" But little did Granny know, that the whole town including the priest, had been viewing my painted look for the past two years! I always got that thrill of being "fly" getting "one over" on my Granny, yes; I was Sleikit, and I loved that.

School leaving day at last. It could not come quick enough and then, the following day back to Ireland for four whole months. And boy, was I going to wow them dead, with my painted face, false hair, false eyelashes, pelmet skirts, skinny rib jumpers on my skinny rib body. Wow, what a picture, a picture alright for the "Hammer House of Horrors!"

Worldly and all, as I appeared, I always had an enormous inner strength of respect for my chastity, there was no way any man nor boy was going to take that away from me. Anyhow, I'd heard boys brag about their latest conquests. Stupid eegits who half the time added their own versions of sex to their stories for effect. No, there was no one taking "that" from me, before marriage at least, for the facts of life even at fifteen, were alien to me. I remember when I came of age, saw my blood; pure panicked, thought I'd haemorrhaged, I thought I was dying after all my dear Grandfather took a cerebral haemorrhage and died. This was happening to me only lower down.

My Granny promptly heard my plea, rushed me off once more to Doctor Travers with a note in my pocket. He, in turn, shoved two sanitary towels in a brown bag and shoved me out the surgery with absolutely no explanation for my horrific mystery illness. Except oh no, "this was going to be a monthly ritual." Heaven help me, for I'd been surely cursed.

On heading straight down the road, and into the local library, I searched and gathered up, various books on "The Facts of Life" and sneakily like an undercover spy, I hid away in a corner of the "reading room" and proceeded to find out for myself just what my mystery illness was all about. Worse still, I was shocked to read it was all in order to have babies. Oh dear God no, with not a maternal nerve in my body. I did not want babies. The very thought petrified me rigid, also, on knowing and seeing women in various states of pregnancy, assured me even more so it was definitely not for me. With stomachs bloated out like big barrage balloons, wobbling along on old flat shoes like wee fat ducks, crying about their sore backs, swollen ankles, and varicose veins, and oh dear God, worse still, allowing any man to visit their private region. Pure degrading, no self respect for themselves. No, to me pregnancy only told the world you let a man 'go there.' Oh heaven forbid that state should ever happen to me. No, I did not need this monthly misery. But worse was yet to come, when I then read in horror, I would suffer this monthly ritual for at least another forty years; this was soon remedied for me though, when my dreaded cycle ended abruptly, due to my chronic anorexia and I liked that.

Tommy still kept in touch, being the only decent boy I'd ever met for the few boyfriends I'd met in the interim were short lived, as the moment they became passionate of within an inch below my waistband, I'd run a mile and quickly end the relationship. Babies, no I definitely did not want them ever, and my own mother and father should have used that advice themselves. For sure for they did not want me either.

Thank God for my Granny, strict and all as she was I really loved her possessively and was so happy she taught me my great self respect and as for boyfriends, I immediately felt disgusted with fear of their groping hands, flaunting their

"Torpedoes of Lust" as I called them fear at the thought of a fat bloated stomach and swollen ankles and with not a maternal bone in my body, fear of the responsibility of another person and worse of all fear of facing my Granny. No, celibacy suited me fine. I liked that.

The summer in Ireland of 1969, my fifteenth year, stands out so vividly in my mind, for two reasons the reason being, that I was viciously attacked and beaten and was surely going to be left for dead without a doubt. And the second reason being I lifted my first drink that same year. Two thoughts will stay uppermost in my mind, two thoughts I shall take to my grave and that being my first drink and my last drink.

But firstly before I touched a drink that summer, I had begged and pleaded with my Granny to allow me to go to the local marquee dance which had been set-up in Moville for the summer season. Knowing my Granny's strictness I knew my pleading would be in vain, as, the dance began at 10pm and ended at 2am. So you can imagine my shock when my Granny one evening permitted me to go to the dance on one condition, I would be home by midnight. I knew rightly not to disobey her curfew, for only a week previous Big Jack the local town heartthrob had asked me out eventually, after all, for years I had prayed he would, and now at last, we had gone to the pictures and I was in my element, only as we came out of the Picture hall the rain came on heavy, so we decided to stand in the shelter of Smiths Shop doorway, where to my delight Big Jack asked to see me again, and made a date with me for the following night. However, from out of the darkness, from nowhere I noticed the faint glow of a flashlight moving towards both us. Then a thud, and a wallop as my Granny from behind the torch, proceeded to batter and bash big Jack about the head and shoulders with her handbag and umbrella, chasing the poor boy for his dear life, then turning on me, gave me the painful treatment all the way back home, forbidding me and grounding me for the remainder of our holiday and needless to say, I never saw Big Jack for dust, from that day to this. So yes, I knew that the very fact that she was allowing me to go the marquee dance that evening was nothing short of a miracle and sure, two hours at the dance was better than nothing, so I knew not to defy her midnight curfew, if I valued my life at all. But ironically, it was due to my Granny's strict curfew that actually saved my life.

On entering the marquee tent, I had a feeling the dance was going to be a disappointment. For a start the band were what I called "ancient" instead of the usual lively popular showband. It was a band of older boys fiddling and rattling button keyed accordions 'old-time', I think it was called with not a soul on the dance floor and even more so, no decent talent coming in the door. As my friend Rosanne and I sat on the bench facing a row of what I unflatteringly termed as 'culchies' with straw in their ears, wellie boots and weather beaten faces. I actually began to think my twelve o'clock curfew was too long to wait for. Also, I had the dread of my road home.

We lived in a very very eerie and remote place in the very outskirts of the town. "Haunted" the locals would say, with the old gate creaking at the top of a very long narrow avenue, fringed by thick bushes at either side, a mile long leading you down over two small bridges where two deep rivers ran. The big house built in the fourteenth hundreds, large, over powering and always in utter darkness, except when I was out only then, would the out light be normally lit for me. My Granny would close the big wooden shutters on every window. Leaving the house itself almost invisible to the naked eye on a dark night. "The dead wont hurt you" my religious Granny would preach. "It's the living" and how right she was. So that's when there and then, at the dance I decided to make my way home. The fear of the dark avenue was bad enough, but the fear of my Granny and her dreaded torchlight was nearly worse. "I'll head for home" I told Rosanne, "there's nothing happening here." And to keep in Granny's good books, I would, for a change be home an hour earlier, and perhaps keep myself in her favour.

Just as I rose to leave the marquee in walked a vision of a dream. Tall, with a halo of dark curly hair, handsome beyond belief. Id never seen him before, a complete stranger in the small town. I promptly sat back down again, pointing out my discovery to Rosanne, who had to agree he was a hunk. With much smiling and batting of my false eyelashes and probably the fact that I had no great competition, I was delighted when my efforts had the desired effect. Over came my Adonis, and asked me so politely to dance. I was in awe, and could not believe it when he spoke in a lovely soft Scottish accent; in my head, already planning to perhaps meet up again, once back home in Scotland. Oh my, an answer to my prayers. "Tony" as he called himself, told me he was Glaswegian. Great, I thought, not too far from my own hometown. It's getting better by the minute as we chatted merrily, laughed and danced, I did notice Rosanne had already left the dance knowing for sure, I was in my seventh heaven. Just then, I discovered to my horror, the time and with panic building up inside me, I realised it was 11.30pm. My Granny's curfew was only half and hour away. Not wishing to sound juvenile, or like some poor frightened Cinderella type, I calmly told Tony that "I would have to get home immediately." I did tell him "My Granny worries about me" and I proceeded to tell him "I had a very unpleasant road to walk home." "No problem" Tony smiled looking deep into my eyes. "I have a car." Wow, better still, I was going to be home sooner. I would certainly take him in home for tea, and my Granny's approval. I did alert him to the fact that my Granny would give him the "third degree", religion, what school he attended, his age, who his people where, what his job was etc. It never failed for every boyfriend who happened to be allowed in over the thresh hold.

Tony laughed and mildly told me he thought he'd meet well within my Granny's approval. This man was an angel, in my eyes; I'd never met such a pleasant person in my life. He truly was "Gods Gift." He led me from the marquee to the carpark where he guided me towards his small yellow mini traveller car. I shall never forget the car because little did I know it would soon become my tomb.

As Tony opened the car door, he took great patience I thought enclosing me "safely in", as he put it. I do remember taking note that there was no interior door handle, but a long plastic string affair, that had to be pulled downward to open the door. I remember commenting on the handle, as the car interior light lit it up, while Tony fiddled around with the window. Anyhow I was too ecstatic to chat about doors, as I eagerly directed Tony on the journey home. "Turn left at the big old gates" as we left the tiny town into the outskirts. "Drive on and on down." Down the avenue, winding and narrow, eerie and pitch dark except for Tony's headlights glaring, lighting up a bit at a time, the creepiness of our route. Only I knew every turning on the avenue, the first wooden bridge the second old stone bridge and as we slowly drove, Tony remarked "Do you actually live down here?" "Oh, yes" I cheerfully replied. "As we go on from the stone bridge, you will come to the house", I assured him. As we got around the last bend of the avenue, my Granny had the whole house in utter darkness. She usually kept at least the outdoor lamp lit. But no, the big shutters, now closed tight, you could but scarcely see the outline of a house at all. "Stop, stop here, we're at the house", but Tony drove on. Straight on past the house towards the area of thick bush which fringed the deep river below. He came to a stop very abruptly, as by now, I couldn't understand this mans mentality. I knew the area so well. I had told him to "Stop at the house" but he deliberately ignored my instructions. Now we were landed in the blackest, darkest remotest part of the grounds in amongst thick trees and bush flanked by the deep river below. As Tony switched of the engine, he sat in total silence for what seemed forever and I really began to feel frightened. "Did you not hear me say the house was back there?" I asked in a quiet civil manner. He did not reply, just stared straight ahead into the black beyond. "If you reverse back you will be able to directly reach the house, and park safely." I now shakily stuttered. Still he said nothing continuing to stare ahead. With total fear and confusion rising in me, I had remembered the old style unusual door string handle, and I nervously fumbled and searched the door in the total darkness, like a blind woman, until I, at last found the plastic string pull. As I pulled down the door string furiously the door would not open. Oh my God he had locked me in. Pure panic began to choke at my throat with a cold sweat and sick roar I began to cry "Let me out", I pleaded "Please let me out!" He still sat trance like beside me. His silence beginning to deafen me as I could actually feel fear pounding even at my very ears; rather than squeal and scream, with not a living soul to hear, would have been pointless.

I started to beg Tony to reverse back, "Come into the house, meet my Granny, have a cup of tea." Good God she wasn't that bad, I half joked in tears. Still no reaction. Tony just continued to look straight ahead, whereby I now furiously tugged on the door handle. The string cutting into my hands. I thought of alternative ways of escape and other than break the window, which was too small, even for my thin frame to crawl from. I knew he meant business. I knew without him saying a word, I was in deep danger as there were only two doors in the vehicle. I looked behind to see the only other doors were two van type doors to the rear of the car, but I would never make it back there to escape with him directly beside me, blocking my exit through, and besides, I knew he would also have those van doors locked. No wonder he took great care to shut me in the car at the dance. He was in fact actually deliberately locking me in on purpose. For what purpose? Oh my God, "Please help me" I cried from the depths of my soul, "Please help me."

Just at that moment, Tony rallied from his trance like state and switched on the car interior light. As he slowly turned towards me, I frantically tried to quieten my sobs, and I once more pleaded for him to let me out. I remember so vividly how his appearance seemed to have changed, even in the dull car interior light. He looked so frightening and menacing. Where was the angelic man? Where was the soft spoken mild mannered, wonderful person I'd met less than an hour ago? No, he was gone, well gone, and I knew there and then, I'd met my own Jekyll and Hyde.

Tony grabbed me by my hair, twisted the polo neck section of my jumper tight around my throat, proceeded to batter my head off the window of my door, continually beating and chocking me by my polo neck sweater twisting it tighter and tighter around my throat. Beating my head furiously in the procedure and pulling me by the throat towards his now furious face. He spoke at last "Your dead meat, your fucking dead." His soft accent menacing into a thick Scottish frightening growl. "I know you're type" he scowled "with your painted face, your come on looks, your teasing ways, Miss Innocent my arse, You're dead lady." By now I was paralysed by fear as he drew his fist back and punched my face repeatedly. I still today shudder to remember my ordeal. I did not struggle, I had no escape. I was no match in strength for this man. So I just had to take this abuse. He menacingly threatened me horrifically with every punch telling me what he was going to do with me, before he'd leave me dead. With blood everywhere from my head and face, my white jumper ripped and stained scarlet, I knew I had no hope. But suddenly Tony stopped hitting me, put his two hands back onto the steering wheel turned to me and growled "I'm going

out to the bog, and when I get back, I'll finish you for good."
This was my only chance, he was going out the vehicle only
just to pee, but he was going out. The car would open I knew
fine my door was well locked but his door would open. As he
opened his door with his right hand, his left hand was still on
the steering wheel and this was my only chance. I grabbed his
left hand and with my tombstone like teeth, I sank and bit
right through his flesh to the bone. I can remember vividly
cutting through his hand fiercely. "You fucking bastard" he
screamed and my teeth stayed buried in his hand. He tugged
his hand free, stumbling out the car door in pain, and I now
on my hands and knees crawled from the car scrambling
furiously to the ground. I ran, got to my feet and ran
screaming frantically as Tony caught me by my hair and tired
to drag me back, pulling and struggling to get me back into
the car. Tearing and ripping the clothes from my body, blood
everywhere, for now his hand was also an open wound. This
was the end. When suddenly, the outhouse light went on
brightly lighting up the way. My Granny appeared at the
front door with a floor brush in hand for armour. Tony, in
pure shock and surprise let go of me. I screamed and ran
towards my Granny, whilst Tony clumsily reversed the mini
traveller at top speed, not knowing any sense of direction,
practically ran over my Granny, who was by now out
swinging and swaying the floor brush down on the rear of the
car. Shouts screams and cries were everywhere in the dead of
the night. It truly was like a scene from a very horrific
nightmare. With his tyres spinning and engine roaring Tony
sped off at top speed up the avenue over the two bridges and
back to where he came from.
My Granny took me limping into the house, did not give out
to me, bathed my head and face, cleaned me of blood but
wouldn't call the police. We had no telephone, but she
refused to involve the law, which I still feel today was wrong.
But although Tony was out there still probably to this day, I

was alive, thanks to my Granny. I never again grumbled about my "fathers buck teeth" nor my "granny's strict curfews". No amount of makeup would camouflage my bruised swollen face and besides I did not care to go dancing or singing and as for men, well, I'd had enough of those. My Granny even started to suggest I go out again that summer, but my depression only grew and my anorexia raged.

I received a letter from home. I sat down and read the contents. It was from my first love Tommy. "When will you be coming home?" He wrote, "I can't wait to see you." I immediately put pen to paper in reply to this letter and told him nicely "We were finished." He was too serious. My 'Dear John' letter certainly did the trick for he did not reply in retaliation and that only proved to me, yes, we were finished. My bruises healed and my face settled back into place, and although I had bald patches where my hair had been torn from my scalp by Tony, I survived, pulled on a wig, painted myself up once more and began to feel slowly better each day. But for me, I could never, ever be thin enough and my Granny was as usual, demented with worry about me.

The final month of the holiday stretched ahead and I perked up when my best friend Patricia decided to come to Donegal for a two week stay. Patricia was so very opposite from me. Solid and reliable she had found a good job from school and remained there for years. Whereby I, came straight from school to my four months holiday. Oh, not to worry I had plenty of time to get a job when I'd return to Greenock. Plenty of time. Patricia arrived and the fun was back in my life. I didn't dwell on my attack, and actually tried to put it behind me and soon enough Patricia and I were eyeing up the local talent, giggling and chatting about who the best hunk was. Once more, I was dancing and even singing again. Yes, Patricia was the tonic I needed. Thank God for her, she was truly my one and only best friend. That was, until when on

that very holiday in my fifteenth year, I discovered alcohol.
Unknown to me then, my mother had started to drink heavily
at fifty years of age. She had never drank, hated what the
stuff did, had already seen so much of it with my father, and
Jaws and as I had the same opinion of alcohol, I would have
been truly shocked to discover my mother was drinking. For
sure, there was nothing worse than a drunk woman. A man
could just about get away with it, but a drunken woman in my
opinion, was the pits.

I had visited pubs before. I wasn't that naive, but never for
drink. My friend, Patricia and I would call in an odd night
before the dance started, to perhaps hear the music or as they
say in Ireland "hear the craic". Anyhow, drink was so very
fattening, loaded with calories. There was no way I could
have that, and besides, I had my Granny to face. Dear God, if
she knew I attended pubs, she would have "swung for me"
without drink! No, I was happy enough to sit in the lounges
and nurse my "soda water" all night. Until, that was, when on
one night in particular, Patricia and I were invited to join a
party of local girls in the Anchor Bar in Moville. We were set
out to go on the Marquee dance, but the girls insisted we join
in the fun. We all sat around a large table in the pub. An
empty glass jug was placed in the centre of the table and each
girl in turn, poured their alcohol into the jug. When it came
to me I mumbled something about me "Just having a soda
water." "Pour it in" they cried, "It will dilute the drink a bit."
Not wishing to be a wet blanket, I proceeded to pour my
drink into the jug. The mixture looked vile, to say the least,
someone stirred it with a big soup spoon and poured each of
us a full glass. I remember as it came around to me, I point
blankly refused to accept the dark mixture. The look of it was
enough. Each in turn kept visiting the bar as round after
round was thrown into the jug, mixed and passed around.
The girls were giggly, jolly, singing and obviously very well
oiled. I remember saying to Patricia "We had better go", for

I knew also, that in the Parochial Hall upstairs from the pub, that my Granny was attending the Chapel Bingo night. "Come on Patricia," I urged, "we want to get a good seat at the dance, before the drunks come out of the pubs." I also knew, and Patricia also knew that if my Granny happened to see me coming out of the Anchor Bar, or any bar for that matter, then "God help me." The concoction came around again and once more, the party urged me on to have a drink. "Try it, that's all, just try one." And as easy as signing my soul over to the devil, which I would have been as well doing, I took the first drink.

Not knowing my fate was sealed at that very moment. I remember the liquid sliding past my throat, down into my stomach, warm and fiery on its journey down and when it hit my very empty stomach then "Wow" where had I been all my life. I hadn't lived at all until now, this feeling was 'Magic'. I looked at the flames of the open fire and they were glittering and dancing up the chimney. I proceeded to look for that feeling of my first drink for many years to come, but never ever did get it again to my peril and high cost. 'Whose round is it now?" I cackled, insisting the jug be re-filled. The girls laughed and joked at my performance as I drank round after round greedily, knocking them back, as if I were an 'old hand' at this drinking lark. After another hour or so, for by now, I had lost trace of time, Patricia urged me now to leave the bar. "Your Granny will be leaving the Bingo hall, I'm so afraid she sees you like this." "Oh shut up Patricia" I slurred. "My Granny doesn't know what she missing." Pioneer, tea total, oh my, a drink is what my Granny needs, I squealed. This was alexia, I could be me. I didn't much care about my painted face, my hair, not to mention my Granny to face.

On eventually being persuaded to leave the bar, in my drunken state, I insisted on going up to the bingo to see my Granny. Patricia had an awful job to try and half carry me to the marquee, where I not only got a seat, but I lay slumped across it for the remainder of the dance. The next thing I remember, was Patricia shaking and trying to wake me up, to get home before my curfew. "Sober up Marilyn, drink this black coffee, please sober up," Patricia was crying at me. "Your Granny will kill you and me." "Ok, Ok, I'm ok," I stuttered and on walking with Patricia on our way home. My fear set in. Unbelievable fear, not of the ghosts in the avenue, not even of being attacked again but an agonising fear of my Granny, and, I sobered up.

On entering the house, my Granny miraculously did not notice any evidence of my drunken escapade. Brilliant, I got one over her I remember my fear easing, as my Granny, the great alcohol detector did not seem any the wiser to my drunken condition. It worked, my inbuilt ability to "appear sober" to the very person I thought I'd never fool. This ability to "appear sober" to my Granny worked for many year's or believe me, reader, I would not be here to tell my story.

The following day I felt great. My flyness, my old sleikit ways were working. I got great pleasure in slyly getting past my Granny's scrutiny and I loved that.

I returned to Greenock eagerly looking for a job, and in those days, jobs were easy enough to come by, so easy that I had nine jobs in a year, ranging from the local wool mill, I only lasted one morning, factory work was definitely not for me. No, shop work was my forte. After all, I'd had enough sales experience all my childhood with my own little makeshift business at home. You could then literally walk into one job one day and into another job the following day. At least I did. I would walk the streets, in and out of every store genuinely looking for work and I was very fortunate indeed with some days being employed on the spot. I remember thinking a chemist shop is more for me. So I tramped through every chemist shop in Greenock until at last, I got a start in a very very old chemist shop named 'Muirs'.

Dismal and drab as I thought the shop, and sorry to say the

owner also. I was delighted that Friday when Mr Muir told me to start on Monday. I rushed home to my Granny with my news which she was by now well used to hearing, "I'll be selling make-up" I screeched. "I'll be making up the medicines for peoples prescriptions, I'll be developing peoples camera spools into photographs for them." Yes, I liked that. My Granny immediately rushed out and bought me a pure white overall from the market, and promptly starched it crisp and white for me. That weekend, I could hardly contain myself for the exciting thoughts of my new job.

Monday morning came at last, except, my Granny put too much starch in my overall and I couldn't bend my arms. On walking up the road to Muirs chemist, I resembled something close to the "Curse of the Mummies Tomb" with my stiff thin body, encased in my Granny's stiff white coat. My pale white face caked in pan stick, dear God I could have haunted the mummies right out the tomb! Anyhow, on entering my new post, I was greeted by Mr. Muirs sad old crabbit face, and worse to come, his assistant, a woman in her very elder years with a face sour and twisted, wrinkled up and bitter. She grunted "Hello" and walked past me into the back shop. Oh no, I was already doubting my new choice of career. Not to worry, I'll soon be behind that counter selling merrily, making people well with my medical concoctions. Right, "Where do you want me to start?" I beamed at dismal Mr. Muir. He in turn disappeared into the back shop and clutching a very long set of ladders, "Get outside and do the windows, you'll get a bucket, chamois, and water from the shop next door." Oh, my this was unexpected. I did not apply for a window cleaning job. Eager enough to please, I obeyed Mr. Muirs instructions and proceeded to try and attempt my task. November in Scotland is to say the least, outer Mongolia with cold and frost and now, not only were my arms too stiff to move in my Granny's starchy overall, but they were now totally stiffened up completely with the cold. Every so often,

Mr. Muir would appear to inspect the job and eventually gave a grunt of approval. "Thanks be," I thought. I'll get in behind the counter at last. "Do the glass inside now" Mr. Muir commanded. As he pointed out the shop fixtures and fittings which were all glass; that may I say, had never if ever seen a chamois never mind a shine. "After that, do the floors and mop the toilet, then you can put the kettle on and make our tea."

Knackered and exhausted I trudged my way home. "How was your first day?" my Granny beamed. "Awful" I signed, "I'm nothing more than a skivvy, I hate it Mum," I replied. "Oh give it a chance" my Granny chuckled. "You've got to start somewhere. Tomorrow's another day."

My Granny was right, give it a chance perhaps tomorrow I'd be selling potions and prescriptions, make-up and photographs. Tuesday came fast and as I entered the house of wax museum (as I called it) I was all set to meet my public.

"Wash out all the old medicine bottles" Mr Muir ordered, head down. "Then carry them all in boxes over the road to Doctor Montgomery's surgery, then carry back the dirty bottles to be washed out tomorrow." What? He wanted a carthorse, not an assistant. It was still only Tuesday! "After dinner, you will be working with the medicines." Great I thought at last, that's more me, only to find to my horror he had me lick and stick labels on prescribed medicines for four hours with my tongue stuck to the roof of my mouth, arms aching, back breaking and even the starch in my stiff overall having withered, I'd had enough.

"Don't ask me about today" I screeched at my Granny "I'm packing that job in. I will put my weeks notice in first thing in the morning." Although how I was going to manage a week more in there was torture to my brain.

My Granny just shook her head, rolled her eyes to the ceiling and for once, she said nothing. Wednesday came and I trudged up the hill to old Muirs Chemist and started to realise the bitter twisted old face went with the job. Dear God, it would not be long until I also had that look. On entering my post I got a "grunt" of "morning" from Mr. Muirs sad old assistant, and as I proceeded through the pharmacy, I was now facing the boss himself, with his unhappy frown. "Mr Muir, could I have a word with you Sir?" "Yes" he grunted under his breath, not even turning to acknowledge me. "What is it?" he mumbled. "Mr Muir, I'm not happy at my work" I chirped, "I would like to put in my one weeks notice." There was complete silence, as the atmosphere thickened with gloom: then Mr Muir crossed to the filing cabinet and desk. He came to me immediately handing me an envelope. "Here's three days wages and your cards, you may well go now! For that matter I do not want anyone in this establishment who is not happy with their work."

Well reader, I looked at the "Gruesome Twosome" as I called them and left there and then for, if this was them happy at their work, I was definitely in the wrong job. I felt a huge weight lift from me as I skipped home, delighted that my short lived pharmaceutical career had ended.

My jobs that year were, as I said, 'many', I still sang; now with local teen pop bands, in the evenings, and in the daytime. I continued to weave my way through half the shop jobs in the town. That is, until I found a job I actually quite liked, working as a trainee window dresser with the local House of Fraser department store. I liked that. Doing displays, dressing the windows was a very nice job. My manager Mr Marshall, was a pleasant enough fellow, in his middle forties. But sadly did not keep too well. He suffered from severe epilepsy and was on constant medication for his illness, but, he taught me how to cope should he ever "fit." Sheer panic struck me at the beginning, but I got well used to Mr. Marshalls illness and I could well cope, with his instruction. We became a good work team he was an excellent window dresser and teacher, and a good manager also. But me as usual although, managing to get my day job right, I still felt I had not accomplished anything with my music and singing in my evening work. "Join my band" mother suggested on one of her rare visits "What? a dance band, with trumpets, fiddles and accordion, no way, that's ancient. Not for me". Fox trots, waltzes and gay gordons, no not for me, I was more Beatles, Stones and Deep Purple. Definitely not for me, was my mothers scene. But with a bit more persuasion, I joined my mother's band. If only just for the grand experience of working with some of the most excellent musicians in the land. My mother got me well known to other bands in the area, and I was now freelance working most evenings. To top it all, one day whilst I was dressing one of the shop windows, a well known local newspaper photographer stopped and approached me and enquired "If I had ever had my own photographs taken professionally?" "Oh, no" I replied, "just the usual box brownie holiday snaps", "I wouldn't want to break your camera" I joked. "If you agree" John said, "I would like to take your pictures for the many newspapers I work on." "What?" I quizzed, "Yes" he said "that's exactly what I mean." "Me, a model," I gasped, for a start my Granny would hit the roof and what about my buck teeth and red face? Anorexic body and poor hair? Some model I'd be, I thought but needless to say, my Granny did not hit the roof, she agreed instantly on meeting John, and I was now peering out from every newspaper in the land. Posing, smiling, "Miss Decimal Day", Miss Inverclyde, Miss This, Miss That, Dolly of the Year, Silhouette of the Year. My God, my buck teeth and high complexion were certainly working in my favour. Now, I had three jobs on the go, but as the books says "No Half Measures" and I liked that.

Busy and all, as I was that year, I felt there was something missing, and that something was I decided, the euphoric feeling I got back in Ireland that night on my holiday when I took that first drink in the Anchor Bar. Yes, that was what was missing from my busy life. Stage work, modelling work, day work etc, no nothing compared to that feeling I got from alcohol, and the only way to recapture that again was for me, more drink and that is just what I needed. That's what was missing.

Still very underage for purchasing alcohol, my flyness was now very focused on only getting my precious liquid. I had many ways of obtaining my alcohol. I knew the bars that would serve me and I had my best friend Patricia to call into off licences for me as she seemed to get past most off licence assistants easily. Now, my crafty and "sleikit" ways, had spilt right on to my alcoholism. I was now hiding bottles in my cabinet in my room, feeling great, swigging away in secret, whilst my Granny slept, not knowing what I was up to. I got that old buzz not only from my drink but from my sheer flyness of once more getting "one over" on my Granny. I still slept in my Granny's room so I had to be extra careful. I would study my hoard of bottles for hours, all empty, except for the one I would swig from. Somebody one evening had introduced me to Contreau orange liqueur. I loved that. It slid down like lemonade and was seventy proof alcohol. I still managed to hide my drunkenness for a long time, still due to absolute fear of my Granny finding out. It was rather like having an illicit affair, only with the bottle. I would get drunk on sheer anticipation of the thought of getting home to my stash, I would take a drink to go for a drink. I managed to do my jobs with great ease, I felt I looked better. I thought I sang better. The only drawbacks were the mornings for my day job. I would be well prepared with aspirin, eye drops, alka seltzer, peppermints oh and not to mention being dowsed in perfume was a classic for me. I had an enormous capacity to hold my drink. I would not eat a bite, and would deliberately drink on an empty stomach. Anyhow, food soaked up drink, and I felt that was such a waste and in my opinion, food and alcohol did not mix well. For the food would only end up vomited out somewhere and once more, wasting the object of my exercise to get drunk. I could never ever understand how people could eat a full three coarse meal, and drink dinner wine as well for all I drank, I never could stomach dinner wine. I felt it was vinegarette jaw-clamping stuff. That for me, took far too long to 'kick-in'. No, I drank for the total effects of the alcohol and nothing especially food, was going to get in its way.

Unknown to me, and very shocked I was to discover then that my mother at this time has also started to drink. A woman whom had hated alcohol for several reasons; her upbringing with my strict tea-total Granny, her failed marriage with my alcoholic father and just general drink and trouble she saw, especially in her show business career. So when joining up with my mother, I was actually very sad to discover that she too, at fifty years of age, had began to drink as much as me. Somehow, the pedestal I had put her on all of my life had slipped, to me, it was alright for myself to get plastered but somehow, it was not right to see my mother drunk. Discovering that my precious mother could match me drink for drink was quite daunting at first, but soon became part and parcel of acceptance to me. That's the thing about alcoholism, the unacceptable soon becomes accepted. Drink would soon tell me that everything normal that was wrong, was really very much right. I was getting away with my secret nightly binges easily enough until one evening I had been out celebrating with my friend Patricia and just drank and drank continual double vodkas the whole evening. On spotting a very dear family friend and her husband in the pub, I decided to join them at their table. The woman, Susan, did comment to me that she thought I was overdoing the drink a bit, and that knowing my Granny I'd have hell to face. After all, I was very much underage. "Oh, chill out Susan, it's a doddle. My Granny hasn't a clue and anyhow, I'll decide when I've had enough not you!" I got up to go to the ladies room and fell flat on my face. I decided to join the band for a song, and made a complete fool of myself with the band telling me to sit down. My friend Patricia actually suggested we get out of the pub, so as I could sober up before having to confront my Granny. Patricia also knew the trouble she would be in from my Granny, for allowing me to get into such a state. Therefore, poor Patricia felt full responsibility for drunken old me. Everyone had to be responsible for me; except me. As Patricia lifted me out of the bar that evening, we both sat for two hours in the fire escape stairway of the local high-rise flats, with Patricia trying in vain to sober me up. "Marilyn, your Granny, think of your Granny, She'll kill you and me, Please sober up." I vomited and came round a bit with my head between my legs, my clothes wrecked, the evening ruined. Sent of the stage by the band, and what did I say to Susan? I was now beginning to feel mortified and worse to come my Granny, I soon sobered up. But as it happens, not enough for although I sailed into the house, straight past my Granny into my bed, my drunken escapade had in no way ended. I began to vomit violently, shake and basically foam at the mouth. Ramble and rant, raving and gibbering, rolling in the bed with my Granny horrified, thinking it had something to do with my severe anorexia.

She called the doctor and called my mother immediately. With cold compresses on my head the doctor gave me an injection. My mother and Jaws, had appeared at my bedside after a two hour journey, not best pleased at now three o'clock in the morning I came around. Only to look at the many faces surrounding my bed, the first face the doctor, saying "She inebriated." The second face, my mother, saying "Will she be alright?" The third face Jaws saying "She's bloody drunk" and horror of horrors the fourth face of my Granny saying "She's dead if she's been drinking, mother of God, I'll kill her." "Tricia" she squealed to my mother "Get the Priest, dear God, get the Priest." My Granny seemed to think the Priest could magically fix anything. So I blurted out the only hope I had of surviving my Granny and the Priest, and that was to "Pass the buck." "It was Susan. I met Susan and her husband in the pub when I only had gone into hear the band. Susan got me drunk. She plied me with vodka." I lied. "Susan did this to me" and God help Susan for my Granny barged right into the supermarket the next morning and pulled Susan over the checkout counter where she worked. Dragged her out to the street and demanded to know the facts and reasons why she had supposedly fed me continual drink! Susan blurted; "She did join us to say hello, but Marilyn was well drunk by then. She was drinking doubles all night, I swear Mrs. L. I had nothing to do with it." Which was perfectly true, and needless to say I got it for sure when my Granny got home and I was dragged to the Priest as well. Also, I lost a good family friend in Susan. Susan came to my place of work the following day angry, rightly so, telling me directly "Marilyn, you're an alcoholic, Nothing but an alcoholic." What? Cheek of Susan calling me that. She's not exactly tee-total herself. Whatever, what a degrading thing to call me. Who'd want her as a friend anyhow? That word, that word 'Alcoholic' I was still only sixteen and trying to enjoy myself, and 'She' calls me an 'Alcoholic', I'll never ever forgive her. Never.

I hated the label 'Alcoholic' and anyone who chose to call me that were totally shunned by me for life. I'll never break breath to Susan again, I vowed.

One morning, not long after that drunken escapade, I got in late to work as usual, and happened to slip, a miniature of vodka in my handbag, just to help 'bring me around' as I called it. When my manger Mr. Marshall happened to walk in on me while I was swallowing my curer. He could I know, have sacked me on the spot. But instead he took me to the staff canteen for a strong black coffee. "Marilyn" he softly began "Please don't think bad of me saying this, but as your manager, I have to tell you straight you're an alcoholic." "What?" I exclaimed, "You too, what is it with you?" I immediately jumped to my defence. "I know your problem Mr Marshall, it's jealously, pure jealously. It's because you hate to see me having fun, and enjoying a drink, when you know, that whilst on your medication, you cannot drink." Mr Marshall looked like I had just hit him with a brick. "That's not true Marilyn" he answered. "I worry about you; you don't eat, and I know you drink on a daily basis." "Oh, do you now" I said cockily, "Well, the worst thing you've ever done is call me an Alcoholic". "You'd have been as well to sack me" and I stormed out of the tea-room in absolute hatred and anger. He's another one I could live without I thought to myself, I'm finished with him. I was so angry that I had my old evil thoughts right away. "If he takes his fits, perhaps I'll be too drunk to help him"; and I never ever forgave Mr. Marshall for classing me as an "alky". I wouldn't speak to him, wouldn't do a hands turn for him at work. Really, he would have been as well to sack me but instead he put up with me for a further eight years, for his sins.

Time passed, and I still managed to conceal my 'secret' from my Granny, that was my only concern, for I did not wish in any way to go through what I took with my previous fiasco. So fear, made me wise enough to be on my guard. But as drink is so cunning, there were many times my Granny should have sussed me out but didn't, and I liked that.
Boyfriends came and went. I was too busy with my work to think of men friends. I still managed to "look alright" for my modelling pictures. Well camouflaged, but painted up, behind my heavy mask of make-up, lay a different story. I still had to "gen" a chap thoroughly through before meeting my Granny. He had to be the same religion (even if he wasn't) he had to be of well known good people (even if he wasn't) and

most importantly, he had to be strictly tea-total. Yes, even if he wasn't. I remember one fellow I took home in particular, to meet my Granny. Dougie, he was twenty seven years or so older than me, very rough, from the wrong side of town, and very fond of a refreshment or three; I had him all fixed up with the correct answers for my Granny's "third degree". I knew from the minute he called for me, it was doomed. He had a "few" firstly for a bit of "Dutch Courage" and he walked into the living room very red-eyed and unsteady. "What age would you be?" my Granny snarled. "Eh, twenty five". "Aye, ten years ago" my Granny growled. "And what religion would you be?" "Eh, the same as yourselves" he slurred "and who are your people?" My Granny continued to query. "What area of the town are you from?" On and on my Granny quizzed Dougie until eventually he lost it. "Do you work? Do you have a trade?" she questioned. "No, I don't" shouted Dougie drunkenly, "I fuckin don't work for I'm only a week out of the jail for urinating the public highway, drunk and disorderly, Missus." Well my Granny and I were both stunned at him. I shrunk within myself, wishing the ground would swallow us up at this outburst. "Get out, get out" my Granny squealed, "You drunken no user. "Get him out of here Marilyn before I'm jailed for my actions" my Granny screeched. That was the end of my short-lived romance with the older man. As he headed head first out the building with my Granny's toe embedded in his posterior.

Joe, was my next catch. This I thought was the real thing. Anyway now I just know he will propose, it's a sure thing. I know he is just waiting for the right moment and that moment came one evening when Joe left me home. He and I stood together on the outside landing of my Granny's flat, and I had a bit too much to drink, but I knew I just knew the moment was right for Joe to propose marriage to me.

"Marilyn" he whispered, I have something to say to you "Yes, oh Yes", I replied, "What is it Joe?" "I'm emigrating" he blurted out. "You're what?" I couldn't believe my ears. "You're emigrating?" "Yes, my love, so this will be our final evening together." "Oh, no, oh no", I cried, tears blinding me. "You can't go, you can't leave me." Shock horror rising inside me. I cried bawled and cried a bit more and just then, Joe lifted my chin carefully in his forefinger and whispered "Marilyn, I'll remember you just the way you look tonight." Oh, no I cried more, as my Granny called me into the house on my curfew. As I ran directly into the bathroom I glanced at my reflection in the mirror and was horrified at what confronted me. My lovely wig with the centre parting had slipped down to the side of my right ear. My false eyelashes had landed on my cheeks and two long black streaks of tears ran a river down my face and neck. Remember me how I looked tonight. How could he forget me, my vision tonight would haunt him forever. How could he possibly forget the way I looked tonight? I even frightened myself with one glance.

My next lumbar was Peter. He seemed a great catch. His father was 'Honest John' the scrap metal merchant so he was of money, the same religion as me, and also suited my Granny's requirements to a tee. Sadly, my gold digging feelings overtook my romantic notions for Peter I'm ashamed to say. Peter was quite a poser in his flashy cars, two to be precise, gold jewels, designer suits etc. Yes, money talked louder than passion for me I'm afraid, when it came to Peter. On meeting with my Granny I did not have much coaching to give Peter. He had all the right criteria for the job of escorting me, as far as my Granny was concerned. She knew his stock, his religion, his people, his trade, practically his inside leg measurements and sock size before I did. So when the evening came to introduce Peter to mum, it was a doddle. As I led Peter into the living room of my Granny's flat, she immediately smiled widely and commented he was like "Out of a bandbox." "Your Honest Johns boy?" "Oh yes, Mrs. L",

Peter replied. "How's the business going?" "Great" says Peter. "You went to St. Mary's School didn't you?" "Yes, I didn't miss Mass on Sunday's". "No drink." Peter was well in there with my Granny. But sadly it was I who had fell out of favour with Peter, quite simply when one day after telling the whole staff members of my employment about my great 'catch', gold jewellery, money flying out of his pockets, two cars, and a caravan. Wow, the ladies in the sales departments were all so eager to see this Adonis.

"Oh, he's calling for me straight from work this evening. You will all see him then." Well reader, at five thirty on the dot, I had all the staff members gathered at the door of the store to see my latest flame draped in his riches, driving perhaps his Merc. Oh yes, I'd show the shop what type of 'good catch' I could get, when, all of a sudden from around the corner, pulling an old horse and cart, edged with balloons, and with an old busman's coat to his ankles whilst blowing on an old horn, was my 'great catch' shouting, "Rags and Bones, Rags and Bones." Toot, Toot, Toot, on his old horn. "C'mon folks, Rags and Bones." Toot, Toot, Toot. Well, while the shop staff fell about in fits of laughter, I was mortified to say the least. How could he? How could he show me up like an old dosser? How could he call at my place of work looking like Steptoe? That's it, I'm finished with him I vowed, and I got the bus home in shame. I was to agree to one more date with Peter after much apologising from him of course, and a good number of presents – bribery. Peter and I decided to go to the Moorings Ballroom dance one Saturday evening in Largs.

I still couldn't quite get over Peters appearance at my shop, and although that Saturday evening he looked like a tailors dummy, I could only see him in his horrific working attire. No although he rated high with my Granny's requirements, my estimation of him had dwindled big time.

The dance was packed and buzzing with people all enjoying

themselves. I didn't bother too much with a lot of drink for a change for I felt under Peter's watchful sober eye, I was out with my Granny. He had that effect on me, purely because I guess he was everything my Granny wanted for me, but not quite what I wanted.

Peters vast family of cousins etc had gathered around our table, all very mafia like, I felt with Peter showing me off like a prize hen, and introducing me to "The Family." Whilst they were all cooing and ahing over me, I spotted from the side of my eye, a very familiar sight indeed for drunkenly in the centre of the dance floor, was, surely not? Yes it was Tommy, remember my first love? But he had changed so very much. I immediately noticed how handsome he was and how stupid I was to end our romance two years ago.

I had to get away from my circle of people, and somehow get Tommy to notice me. When the song ended and the dancers sat at their tables, I made an excuse to Peter and my party and crossed the floor towards Tommy's direction. He did notice me eventually and although I felt he was "well oiled" with drink, I was still anxious to say "Hello" and who was I to judge any drunk? "Oh hello" I flashed my teeth in a big grin, as though I'd only just noticed him. "Long time no see" I casually commented. Trying to appear indifferent, but really my heart pounding with fear of rejection. For Tommy also had his own party of people with him, and I noticed a female quite close to hand, and don't forget my "Dear John" letter I sent him from Ireland to finish our relationship. So I waited with baited breath to see his reaction.

"Marilyn, how are you. It's been a long time right enough. You look well." "So do you" I honestly replied. For he certainly looked very well to me even with his slightly slurred comments. So not wishing to overstay my time, I said I had to get back to my party table for as I glanced back, I could see Peter and his cousins getting very anxious looking for me. I made my goodbyes and headed for the ladies room, thinking how well Tommy had looked. "I was a fool to end our relationship" I said to myself in the mirror. Oh well, my loss. As I then came out of the Ladies room, Tommy was stood there waiting for me with his phone number clutched in his hand. He pressed the small note into my hand and said "Phone me tomorrow" and with that, Peters cousins came on the scene to "rescue me" back to their table.

Tomorrow couldn't come quick enough for me. I got myself all prepared for my phonecall. I would no way normally phone any man first. I was always too proud for that, but in this instance it was different. As I dialled Tommy's number, the telephone was quickly answered by his mother, who told me he was out and she would pass on my message and phone number to him when he returned. Oh, no, perhaps he was out with that female from the dance, or worse still, perhaps he was never home yet from the dance. My head spinning with my imagination working overtime, when the phone rang and it was Tommy. We made a date for that very evening and excitement surged through me when he collected me and off we went to the cafe, of all placed. "What about the pub" I said. "Oh, no, no drink, I want to face your Granny with us both sober." Face my Granny I thought to myself, it's too soon, it's far too soon, I panicked inwardly for sure, the one and only time he had faced my Granny, she threw him out of the house and down the close stairs. Close by the way, is the name used in Scotland for the stairwell leading to a tenement flat. How could I produce him to her this evening yet again. No, it's far too soon for that fate! His next question nearly floored me more. "Marilyn, I wont let you go again, will you marry me?" Eh, dear God that's quick work, am I hearing right? "Marry you" I gasped, "sure I've only just met you again" I croaked. "Is it not a bit soon for proposing? Anyhow marriages don't work" I stated. "I've seen to many folks split up, even my mothers marriage didn't work." No marriage would not be for me. At eighteen, I had too many mountains to climb, too many rivers to cross, and too many careers to fulfil. Holy Moly, if I were in fear to introduce him to my Granny as a friend, how in under God could I introduce him as my 'Fiancée'? "She would die with her leg up if she didn't swing for me first". "Café, be damned, We're going to the pub" I quoted "Think I need a drink."

My first date with Tommy went very nicely. I managed to sit nursing my first drink unusually for me, while he declared his undying love for me, and had even forgave me for my "Dear John" letter from Ireland. He told me "He knew I'd return and fate meant us to be together" and that he wanted us to be married and would not take no for an answer. This was all too premature and sudden for me, marriage, no, definitely not for me. So I proceeded to swallow down my large vodka, then another, then another, and once more, Tommy attempted his proposal. "Marilyn, I'll ask you again, will you marry me?" "Och, alright I will" I spurted out. "Hurry up back to the bar" I giggled, "Its nearly last call, same again" as I proceeded to swallow his weeks wages 'No Half Measures'.

Tommy left me home, and decided it was right not to face my Granny yet. "I'll have to break the news to her gently" I said. "We will get engaged, firstly and then I can let her know in my own time" I said. "Great" Tommy replied. "I'll pick you up from work tomorrow and we can go looking for an engagement ring for you." "I have my own transport" he continued. Well for a moment awful thoughts of Peters four legged transport flashed through my head. "Lovely" I answered "see you then."

I got in home safe enough, and lay awake thinking of my future wedding. Yes, I did love Tommy, and no, my Granny would just have to accept him, whether she liked it or not. Tommy was the boy for me and nothing or no one not even my Granny would change that. I was going to have to be firm and stand my ground. I was after all getting engaged tomorrow in my lunch hour and I'd let my Granny know, eventually, maybe, we'd see.

I was very excited at work all morning now telling the full sales staff about my new man and the good news of my forth coming engagement. Although, I was keen not to line them up to meet my new beau, as I still did not feel secure enough after Peter's spectacular arrival. I played down Tommy's arrival significantly, that is, until I heard the roar of an engine drive up to the shop doorway, and instead of four legs, it had two wheels. Tommy had a motorbike. Once more the shop staff gathered like something from 'Grace Brothers' to see my latest flame. I stood gunked and speechless as Tommy kissed my cheek, and handed me a crash helmet and goggles. Oh my God, what do I do with these?

I proceeded to squeeze the helmet over my wig, and that was not easy, and then the goggles came next, and they would not fit over my false eyelashes. Horror, I felt sick, as I glanced at my reflection in the store window and can only say I resembled something along the lines of "Fearless Fly." I'd never been on a motorbike before, and Tommy reassured me to "hold on." As we sped off, with the shop staff waving in the distance, speeding along, I was terrified to say the least, not, may I add, of falling off the bike, but terrified my spare bits would fly off in the wind. My hair, my eyelashes, as my ankles scuffed the pavements on the sharp bends, Tommy squealed from upfront, "Lean with the bike" and the only thought then in my head was, "I only hope, if I fall off, that I hit the ground, before my parts". They would be picking me up in bits, spare bits for I could imagine them finding my hair at the top of Hamilton Street and my eyelashes at the bottom of High Street. Oh God, I can pick them, but I loved him.

Tommy bought me the most beautiful sapphire and diamond white gold engagement ring that very day, and I was delighted, flashing my jewel on my finger, I couldn't wait to show it off, back at the department store. My Aunt Cathie also worked in the store, so I had to be careful not to let her know for as far as I was concerned, Cathie was very much part of my Granny's circle of spies. No, I'd hide my new engagement ring instead for a while anyhow, until I could bravely pluck up the courage to tell my Granny. So now, not only was I hiding food, and drink I was hiding my engagement ring and hiding Tommy as well from my Granny's scrutiny. This idea worked well for two weeks until one day, I got home only to find my Granny standing waiting for me in the hallway, arms folded across her very large chest. I called it the "Gestapo look" and she proceeded to scream. "Engaged, engaged, your bloody engaged. I've to meet a neighbour in the street, who would tell me you're engaged, a neighbour, a neighbour tells me, you bitch, you fly bitch, who is he?" "I'll swing for you both," she squealed, pushing me into the living room she ranted. "Give me the ring, I'll burn it, give me the damn ring, you'll not defy me lady" she wrenched. "Oh no, please God" I thought "Don't let her get the Priest." "I'll phone our Tricia and tell her your performance". "She's your mother and she can deal with you this time. You've broke my heart," my Granny whined. "Broke my heart". "I've did my best to bring you up, with no father at your back, I've did my best and this is how you repay me. I've not even met the pigs get; I didn't even know you were going out with anybody. Who is he? Who is he?" she creamed. "God's curse him." Dear God, I only got engaged, you would have thought I sold my soul to the devil. My Granny was impossible, but I remembered my vow, that I was going to stick to my guns and be firm.

"No, I'm not giving you my ring to put in the fire" I said calmly, and proceeded to tell her Tommy's name. "Him" she screamed, "Him, I threw out?" "You're going to marry him?" "Well, you're dafter than I thought. Oh, God I'm finished, I'm finished, this'll finish me this time" she cried out dramatically. Whilst I still kept my determination strong and knew that my Granny would some day accept Tommy. She'd have to, for I knew he would be my husband, come hell, or high water or even the wrath of my Granny. We would be married.

Eventually I talked my Granny into actually meeting Tommy, and being properly introduced to each other. There didn't seem to be any barriers to overcome or any tuition to give Tommy on my Granny's inquisition. For Tommy was a sure thing. He had all the requirements my Granny had planned for me. He was the right colour, right religion, and of excellent good living people, and although he was drunk the evening I spotted him at the dance, Tommy really did not care for alcohol in general. The only obstacle against his factor was the motorbike, but we would hide the bike until a much later date. For no way could I ever produce Tommy and a motorbike to my Granny in the same breath.

However, the day came for the big introduction and as I led Tommy into the house, my Granny sullenly shook his hand, and welcomed him as best she could, then, sat us in the living room like two bookends, whilst she excused herself to the toilet saying "When I get back, I shall put the kettle on for tea, then I can know more about you." Away she went to the toilet, while Tommy very nervously glanced at me, his stiff collar and tie nearly choking him, and his best suit (his only suit) wrapped round him like an Easter egg, a bit like George waiting to meet the dragon. Back appeared my Granny, drying her hands on a clean towel. Chatting now to Tommy about what area did he live? what school would that be?, what was his job? did he have a trade? As Tommy begun delivering his answers as best he could, my Granny turned on her heels and proceeded to walk away from us, out into the facing kitchen to presumably put the kettle on, when to our shock horror were to discover that while in the bathroom, my Granny had accidentally left the complete back area of her skirt tucked tight, into her big pink winceyette bloomers. What a sight to behold! Now, these knickers would have sailed the Titanic to safety.

Well, by now with my Granny, still chatting as she worked eagerly with tea cups, and biscuits, poor Tommy's face had now lit up bright purple with embarrassment. He pleaded for me to tell her, please tell her. I was doubled over in laughter and said to Tommy "No, I won't tell her." "You tell her!" "No way" he scowled "I want to get out of here alive, please tell her Marilyn." "No", I replied in fits of giggles, "I'll leave it be for a wee while yet." I was having too much fun to tell her. I let her continue to question Tommy while she appeared back and forward with tea, biscuits, sandwiches, spreading things out onto the coffee table in front of us and wobbling back off into the kitchen with the big pink blamanage on full show. Eventually, as she made her final journey to the table, stressing to Tommy, the importance of having a trade, the evils of alcohol and the sacrilege of missing Mass on a Sunday, I suddenly butted in, and chimed out "Mum, your skirt is tucked into your drawers, by the way." Well, she gazed at her behind "Mother of God, you Bitch! I'm affronted, affronted, you let me walk about like that and especially in front of this fellow!" This fellow, whom by now, really did not know where to look. Suddenly, as she hauled her skirt tail out, we all burst into uncontrollable laughter, for believe it or not, my Granny had a sense of humour as well; and now the ice was well and truly broken, for she was to grow to love Tommy like a son. I firmly believe God sent her skirt in the wrong direction for a purpose.

My Granny was getting older and I was becoming stronger in getting my own way with her. Until that is, on one evening, Tommy and I had been out partying, with me drinking continually all night long and demanding we get the late bus to the Moorings dancing where we had met. Tommy pleaded with me to stop drinking, sober up, he'd have to face taking me home. and I non –politely told him to 'shut up', 'get me to the dance'. As we boarded the bus, I produced a bottle of cheap wine from my very large handbag, and proceeded to drink it. I just could not stop, and would not stop drinking, and no one could reason with me. So I finished the wine by the time the bus pulled into Largs, and determined to be first off the bus, I ran unsteadily up the aisle of the bus while the bus was still in motion, and fell face first off the moving vehicle, onto the concrete road below, right down on the right side of my face with my jaw and head taking the full force of the fall. The next thing I remember, was someone shouting for an ambulance and dragging me from the middle of the road onto the pavement. "No, No" I cried, "I'll be alright, leave me alone, I'm going to the dance, leave me alone." I struggled to my feet; half crawled into a nearby telephone booth, and dragged myself up into the dim light of the phone booth, only to be confronted with my reflection in the old worn out mirror of the phone box. My face was busted all down the right side, blood pouring out, eye shut over where the swelling ballooned out of control, my face was totally shattered. Unrecognisable, but I just wiped the blood and told myself I'd be ok when I got to the dance, and would get a drink to steady me. "Where's Tommy?" I drunkenly remembered he was with me. When I suddenly noticed, he had been surrounded by four angry men, shoving and accusing him of beating me up. I staggered over and told them "No", I fell off the bus which took some persuading, until they eventually let Tommy go from their grasp, leaving Tommy on the ground at my feet, they finally walked off in the direction of the dancehall.

Tommy got to his feet, seeing my smashed face in the dim streetlight. He began to cry in despair. "Your face, oh dear God Marilyn, have you seen what you've done to yourself?" "You need to go to the hospital" he cried. "Oh shut up" I snapped, "I'm going to the dance, stop fussing over me." "I will be alright when I get to the dance" I slurred. I proceeded to stagger over towards the dancehall, where immediately two large doormen stopped me in my tracks. "Your hurt miss, very badly hurt, you need an ambulance and you're very drunk." "Oh, not you too, telling me off," Aren't I ruled by bosses, telling me off continually." Now these two morons would not let me in the dancehall door. Tommy pleaded with me to go to the hospital "No way" I growled, soaking up blood with my neck scarf. "I'm going home" I screeched. "No" he demanded. "No, you cannot go home in that state." "Watch me" I cockily replied. As I put out my thumb to hitch a lift, a car stopped abruptly and I got in, leaving Tommy standing alone in the street. I knew I had been viciously attacked before in a strange car, but the drink in me told me I had to get home for my Granny's curfew. Tommy or not, but, unknown to me, Tommy was helped by a friend who told him he would take him in his car to follow me home to safety.

On my drunken trip home, I discovered a very decent polite young man had lifted me. "This is my fathers car" he beamed. "He got it this morning." As he chatted aimlessly about himself and his fathers car, I found it hard enough to see through my swollen eye and with me now in great pain with my shattered face, as the alcohol was wearing off, my feelings were slowly returning. I knew by now, I needed medical help. I was in agony and did not dare look in a mirror. I knew I had done serious damage to myself in the fall.

The driver boy kept chatting on about his family, while I tried in vain to keep my blood from dripping onto his father's new car. And thankfully he drove me straight home, and just as I turned to say thank you to him, a boot came through his side of the door with Tommy's leg attached to it. The new car was wrecked totally. Tommy in worry and anger appeared out of the blue and he pulled the poor boy from the driver's seat onto the ground with me screaming "Leave him alone, he kindly gave me a lift. Leave him alone."

Sadly I never knew the boy or met him since, but I'm sure he'd have some explaining to do to do to his father on returning the new car home. Tommy shoved me into the entrance of my Granny's flat, and scolded me again for hitch hiking. "You're drunk. You're injured and you know the dangers of what you did. How can I take you to face your Granny?" Tommy was actually crying. "Sober up Marilyn, you'll have to go to the hospital. Your face is totally mangled."

I pushed past him up to the stairway and got my key out to get in without my Granny's detection. But just as I turned the key in the door, my Granny opened it from behind. "Oh Mother of God, what's happened to you" she shrieked whereby now Tommy at my side, she also immediately blamed him for my state. "You've hit her, you swine, you've hit her. I'll swing for you." "Cathie" she screamed to my Aunt, "Get an ambulance." Cathie duly phoned 999 and ordered me an emergency ambulance. Coming to clean me up, she spat into my face "You're an alcoholic nothing but an alcoholic" and I was totally enraged by those words. She was the second person to tell me that and I was finished with her for sure. She won't call me an alcoholic I fumed, I'll never ever break breath to her again, I vowed. I kept my oath. I never spoke to her again for a full five years. Later I wouldn't even invite her to my wedding and she lived with me. No I was sick of being labelled an 'alcoholic' by those ones that could drink enough themselves. "She stores a bottle of Sanatogene wine for medicinal purposes" she would say. Medicinal my arse. She could swallow a large refreshment or two, who was she to call me an alcoholic? No, I was finished with her, for sure.

The doctors mended my smashed face where x-rays showed thankfully I had not broken any facial bones. Only, how I had managed not to, I shall never know. My Granny always had maintained Tommy hit me, but maybe it was her way of dealing with my drunkenness that night.

I moved out of my Granny's house, only to land in on Tommy's poor parent's home, with my suitcase (full of bottles). It did upset my Granny terribly, but now I had a free licence to drink where and when I chose. It was breaking my Granny's heart, but I felt I had to 'fly the nest' for I was to be married soon and I'd be gone anyhow. But with my Granny telephoning me continually begging me to come home, I eventually went home on my terms. Monday to Friday staying with my Granny and weekends well, they were at Tommy's parents where I could run riot. They were an elderly lovely couple who really did not realise the degree of my drinking. I had my very own room at their place. Tommy also, had his own room, so everything was very above board in that respect. But not my drinking, especially at these weekends I was out of my Granny's curfew. Out of my head too, with alcohol, and I loved that.

My wedding was approaching rapidly and I was wishing it were all over. With having no money, no father at my back, as my Granny would say. Therefore there was no way I could have a big wedding and besides, I did not want a big do. But unfortunately, my future mother in law did. She wanted, rightly so, her only son, to be wed in style, and decided to pay for the "Full Monty". I truly loved Tommy's mother and father and let his mother take full charge with arguments over "top table" guests and my Granny saying "She would not go to the wedding unless she chose her top table." I was delighted to sit it out and let them all get on with it.

I chose my friend Patricia as my bridesmaid and she and I took the day off work to go into Glasgow to hire her bridesmaid dress and to pay for and collect Tommie's gold wedding ring for the big day. Excited by our day out, I do remember Patricia and me getting to the hire shop, and collecting her dress then, I decided when the pubs opened at 11 a.m. we would call into the famous Glasgow pub "The

Muscular Arms" for just one wee drink "on me" of course. One drink never was enough for me, I proceeded to drink and drink and then, buy everyone in the pub drinks to celebrate with me. Patricia did say several times, "Marilyn we should go now. You have to get to the jewellers shop for Tommy's ring and then don't forget, you have to get home to face your Granny. We should go now." "Oh, we should go now, oh Patricia enjoy yourself, drink up, let yourself go a bit. More doubles over here please."

Closing time came in the pub at 2pm and the last thing I remember was falling down every stair of the pub entrance onto the street, blaming my platform shoes which had broken away totally from my feet. I proceeded to stagger through the streets of Glasgow centre on my bare feet. My shoes in my hand, my tights torn up my legs, what a sight. Patricia tried to help me, but I insisted on going to Sasha Shoe shop for new shoes were therein, the manager told me "Leave the store immediately". "I was drunk and disorderly" and "he would get the police". "Oh shut your effing face up" I squealed, "I'm getting married, chill out a bit". "Have you ever had a liquid lunch? Perhaps that's what's wrong with you." I cheeked and swore at the manager, who promptly threw me from the shop floor out the door onto the street.

"Get up Marilyn, get up" Patricia's voice rang in my ears. "Tommy's wedding ring" I croaked, "I'll have to collect it now." I proceeded to sing and stagger onto the Jewellers shop and vaguely remember not having the money for the gold ring. I had drunk Tommy's wedding ring money in the pub. Between my own greed, and buying strangers drinks, I could not believe I had no money for his ring. I cancelled the gold ring immediately, and let Patricia lead me from the shop whereby, I staggered into Woolworths, still in bare feet, torn clothes and I bought a wee cheap gents silver ring with the last twelve pounds I possessed. "That'll do him fine" I slurred, "a rings a ring, it's the thought that counts" and

Patricia got me into café for a strong black coffee and tried to get home safely past my usual curfew.

I remember vomiting on the train journey home and insisting that my shoes were to blame for my bruises. But not being able to reason with me, Patricia just agreed, moving us to another part of the train away from my sick mess. As I arrived at my train stop, Tommy was religiously waiting for me on the platform. I half fell off the train, waving my shoes above my head, "Hello Tommy, I got your ring, look," I beamed, "Its silver with a nice black stone". "Silvers all the style, who needs gold?. It's too old fashioned these days and look, I fell of these bloody shoes, the platform soles to blame, too high." But as Tommy took a look at me, I knew he was thinking. It wasn't those shoes that were too high. Tommy knew from the word go that he was marrying a drunk and an anorexic drunk into the bargain, but he loved me unconditionally, and I suppose he thought he could change me, once we were married and on our own, but sadly that was not to be after all, for with me, there were definitely 'No Half Measures'.

My mother, by now had her own alcoholic life. She was well flown from my Granny's nest, and she and Jaws were in their own drunken rut. I would see her more regularly now, for at last, we had something in common, drink. She was the one person I knew who could match me drink for drink, not may I add a proud thing to recall your mother for, but we had a very strange closeness now. That only happens through alcoholism, and then, a sudden drastic change would appear in me, and I would actually hate her for deserting me throughout the years. The music would stop, and the fighting and the arguing would start and that was pure hell on earth. I was so unpredictable in drink. I would be full of life and the soul of the party and was invited to many many parties with my guitar, electric piano, songs and laughter abound. Yes, I was the party. While everyone's "bottle" would be given to the hostess, and put into the kitchen bar, to share, my bottle would stay by me, for me, and when I would have it rapidly swallowed, I, then would be in the kitchen bar drinking everybody elses. So selfish for drink, but then, if anyone even passed a slight complimentary remark about my jewellery or coat, or shoes, I would promptly take the item off my back and promptly give it to them to keep. I was one minute the angel of mercy, and the next the devil himself. I truly could make Jekyll and Hyde seem like Tom and Gerry. I was the nicest person you could ever wish to meet and also the worst enemy you could ever have the misfortunate to know. Not only did I have two faces, but I had around forty faces for every dilemma and situation which I would most certainly create. My flyness and slyness grew as rapidly as my alcoholism. They went hand in hand, and I liked that.

With my forthcoming wedding looming closer, and closer, I was becoming even more and more disinterested with the arrangements with my future mother in law taking over and my Granny demanding my Uncle Duncan give me away, and my mother telling me "Jaws" would give me away. I was becoming quite demented with the whole scenario with my Granny threatening not to come, if "Jaws" was going and arguing about top tables. Who should, and should not be invited, I honestly felt I was no part of the occasion at all, not to mention I was only the bride.

Panic struck however, when one week before my big day, I was at work when my work colleague happened to mention wedding licence. "What wedding licence?" I gasped. "You should have applied for your wedding licence about one month ago" she said. "Marilyn you cannot possibly be married without a licence." Oh, dear God, I knew nothing about applying for a licence or calling bans etc, for after all I'd never been married before. I squealed at her "What will I do?" "I've a big venue booked, guests, flowers, cars, photographer, catering, band, what will I do?" Tommy appeared at my workplace just then, and I cried to him "We need a licence." "Eeh" he replied, looking just as panicked and puzzled as me. "A lawyer, we will have to see a lawyer now", I shouted as I reached for my coat and just squealed to my manager I had to go now, to a lawyer, with no thought for my job or anyone. I rushed out the door with Tommy on my arm, to find a solicitor to help us. But firstly a drink, to get my thoughts together, with as usual one becoming two, three, and so on Eventually Tommy begging me to remove myself from the pub, we then started to search for help. We walked rapidly to the west end of town where all the lawyers offices were situated and truly just like I used to do when job hunting or pub crawling we went into every office on that street with no joy. Until one solicitor decided to see us.

I had sobered up quite sufficiently to bluff my interview with him, and on explaining our dilemma through tears and panic, the solicitor seemed to take pity on us and made a few short phone calls meantime, telling us to accompany him to the local Greenock Sherriff's Court. Oh, dear God, I didn't like the sound of that one bit, but we had little or no option so were led along the road in the lawyers large car to court.

On arriving in the court room, I realised I recognised the main man himself. Sherriff Patrick was a very strict, stern unapproachable feared man in the law community and I would have to be facing him today, a fate worse than my Granny. Still, Tom and I were sworn in turn to take the stand, bible, oath etc and explain our situation. Tommy did alright with his explanation of just truly not knowing anything about applying for the licence and explaining to Sherriff Patrick how sorry he was to take his time, and how grateful he was for the Sherriff seeing us. Anyhow, I came to the stand next and my pleading face was automatically put on show. "Why should I grant you a licence?" said Sherriff Patrick, peering down at me through half cut glasses perched on the edge of his nose. "What makes you any different from anyone else?" "You made the error of not applying for the licence in the first place," he grunted, "so why should I grant you a 'special licence'?" "I've got to get married" I squealed at him holding my stomach in the process. "What?" he exclaimed, "Do you mean you are pregnant?" "No" I shrieked, "I mean, I've got to get married for I've got the bloody half of Greenock coming to my wedding and if I'm not there, what's the guests, taxies, flowers, caterers, band, and priest going to do?" Oh my god, the Priest would need to be cancelled. My Granny would kill me this time for sure. It didn't bear thinking about. "If there isn't a wedding next Saturday with me in it" I cried, "there will be a funeral with me definitely in it. You have to help us please," I said. Sherriff Patrick told me abruptly to sit back down in the courtroom and keep quiet.

Tom drew me a warning look, to shut my mouth and I managed to stay silent for a short while until of course Sherriff Patrick came back through with his decision on our licence dilemma. As he sat himself back onto his high chair he very sternly addressed us once more, over his little spectacles saying "The licence I would be granting today is a very special licence for military and sea-going people only" and before he could get another word out I suddenly stood up with a jolt shouting "But Sherriff, I've been to sea, I worked on the Waverley for a week three years ago, up and doon the Clyde, round the three lochs, the Kyles of Bute, Gourock to Dunoon, Rothesay and even two trips to Millport, I've been to sea alright." "Will you be quiet" Sherriff Patrick once more warned me, "If you don't shut up, you'll be locked up." Tommy was cringing in his seat and very angry with me indeed. But thankfully, my licence was granted that day, I'm sure of sheer pity for Tommy with Sherriff Patrick wishing him well for after all, he'd need his best wishes marrying me. It wouldn't be a licence he would need, it would be a medal.

With our special licence in tow, we happily paid the pricey sum of twenty pounds and went on our way. "Money well spent" I thought.

The night before my wedding the phone rang and it was mother very drunk. "I'm not going to your wedding tomorrow, I think I'm taking the flu" she slurred. "What" I cried, "please don't do this to me Tricia, please come to my wedding." I could not take any more blows, I dropped the telephone receiver, whereby my Aunt Cathie saw my stress and although we were not on speaking terms for years, promptly took the receiver, and summoned my mother to "Be at the wedding tomorrow, with no more nonsense, just be there!" And sure enough my mother did appear for my wedding after all, with she and I actually getting through it relatively sober too. It was quite a triumph for us both. Even although very much against my Granny's wishes, Jaws did get to give me away; the big do went well on the day after all thank God.

We had two weeks honeymoon in Blackpool which went well. I love Blackpool to this day, and I had many drinking holes in that town, Yates Wine lodge being my favourite. I truly loved that place, with drinking stalls, stone floor, an almost old market atmosphere which I felt so at home in, mixing fancy cocktails at one stall, moving onto beer at another, on then to spirits stall, and so on and on an on. I would seldom have to leave that wine lodge all day and night. I practically lived my two weeks in Yates. And that, to my idea was a honeymoon made in heaven.

On returning home we made ourselves at home in the tiny one bed attic house we had bought with a loan from the council. We were very happy indeed, and although my drinking was very heavy, Tommy just accepted it as part of me, and would buy me drink constantly for a quiet life, rather than refuse me and face hell.

I still miraculously managed to hold my window dressing job

down only just, as I know I was being watched carefully by the new management. But my flyness and sheer luck let me away on many drunken occasions at that job. With money very tight indeed, every penny we earned would be drank by me, and although we both had good paying jobs, there was never enough money to cover my habit. I justified my daily drinking to Tommy quite simply when he suggested "just drink at the weekend Marilyn." I decided no, because "Listen Tommy," I would slyly crawl round him, "Why pack all that drink into a weekend, when I just have to spread it out every night?" But in reality, I was spreading a weekends drinking into every night instead. I celebrated Hogmanay every night. I never ever got to handle our money. Housekeeping, cooking etc was all down to Tommy, especially since the one and only time Tommy entrusted me to pay the monthly mortgage. That morning he carefully counted out the mortgage money with the payment book and all my instructions. "In your lunch hour, go straight to the council offices, pay in the money directly". "Get the book stamped and receipted." "For God's sake you'd think I was five years old" I squealed. "I know how to pay a bill. Give me the damn thing to pay. I'll be fine, trust me please." "Och, your right love" he said hugging me close to him. "Of course I trust you, after all it is the roof over our head at stake." Tommy forever the pessimist always had to see things all black of course he could trust me, couldn't he?

My lunch break came at last, at my work and I only had to cross the road to the town council offices to pay the mortgage but sadly I also had to pass by the "Jolly Sailor" pub on my journey. "One wee drink wouldn't matter, and I had the mortgage money separate anyhow, I deserve one wee drink, it is my dinner hour after all."

I was fly and careful enough to try and control my drinking in the pub for I did have my job to return to. But, as I started to make my plans to leave the pub, horror, and a panic struck me as I got through my third drink. "Oh no, I've broken into the mortgage money," I said to the barmaid, "I'll have to go an fix it" and truly, full of all the right intentions, I felt there was no sense in going to pay the bill with a chunk of the money gone. So I proceeded into Haddows Off licence shop, and stocked myself up with four bottles of vodka, and as many cans of beer and with no thought at all to the mortgage. I then went next door to "Paiges" clothes shop and kitted myself out with a new two piece suit and a coat to match from their sale. As I struggled home that evening with all my purchases, I could only think of how nice Tommy would think I looked in my new outfits and bargains.

Tommy stared at me as I squealed my way into our tiny hallway with my big cargo of drink and my many purchases. "Did you get the mortgage paid?" he gasped in despair. "Ehh, oh no, Tommy I didn't, but I did get some lovely new gear". "Fetch a tumbler and I'll pour us a drink to celebrate." I shall never ever forget the anger and disbelief that became a mask immediately over Tommy's face. Not to mention the unrepeatable mouthful he gave me in return. With no savings, no spare cash to our name, Tommy had some explaining to do to the town council to excuse the missed payment. Needless to say, I've never to this day been given a bill to pay again.

My drink came before anything in my life. It came first and foremost. How to get it, how to get the money to buy it. Earning money was never a problem to me, working was something I simply had to be good at. But it was getting me there, and relying on me that was my employer's problem. I was getting more sick daily with hangovers, time keeping, and no respect for management whatsoever. I was truly a law unto myself, and how I got away with it in jobs, I'll never know. But I did for many years to come. Camouflage was my middle name, with my paint, powder, wigs, false eyelashes, eye drops, and mouth fresheners. I still miraculously managed to do my modelling work, and believe me, the camera does lie, for if the camera could have truly seen even an inch beneath my mask, the only modelling I'd have done would have been wanted posters for the House of Usher.

Although I prided myself on holding enormous amounts of alcohol, I still had horrific accidents whilst drunk. Like the night I fell down head first the full spiral stairway to our house. Every stair I smashed myself off and lay at the bottom with my neck and chin opened wide from ear to ear, blood pouring from me and as usual, faithful Tommy there to get me to hospital again. It was always my face I fell on. How could I not wreck my arms or legs in my sick mind. Why was it always my face? I can vividly remember the doctor that night telling me "I was drunk" and as he examined my torn face with the bottom half of my chin and neck area were open like two mouths, I remember as he began to stitch and sew me up, I cockily said to him "Do a good job, I've to get pictures taken for my modelling job from this face". "Make the scar below my chin small". "Don't be putting in big knitting needle stitches," as I instructed him continually. I know to this day as he begun to sew me, he really felt like stitching up my big mouth at the same time to shut me up for good

I remember the first few stitches and then I passed out completely, only coming around in the morning, in a hospital bed and the usual horrific flashbacks to my ordeal last night. Where had I been? What had I done? – Blackouts. I staggered from the hospital bed to the toilet, terrified to confront the damage I'd done. I knew my face was in a very bad shape, for I could not speak or open my mouth at all, and as I slowly looked in the mirror, I was shocked to see my chin and neck swollen like a black balloon. A row of blood hardened stitches under my chin presumably holding my chin to my neck area together.

A nurse promptly appeared summoning me back to my bed. Whereby, I shook her off, retrieved my clothes from my locker and signed myself out of the hospital against doctors suggestions and orders, right into the nearest pub to the hospital I could find. I was so desperate for a drink, that knowing I could not put a class to my mouth with my injuries, I promptly got a straw and proceeded to suck my vodka up through the drinking straw, enabling me to still drink greedily sore face or not. I would not be beaten by a row of stitches. How desperate was I?

My face healed once more and once more Tommy's nagging me to cut down on alcohol truly annoyed me. "No wonder I drink" I'd cry to him in retaliation, "Married to you! Nag, nag nag". "Bosses at work, bosses at home. I'm sick of it. No wonder I drink." I defended every drink I ever took even to the very end of my drinking career.

"We'll move house" I suggested, "Stuck up here in the attic would make anyone drink". So, we sold our little attic and moved to what was to become our house of hell.

I remember the day I first seen what I thought, was to seriously be our dream home. The house had lay empty for thirty years, but building contractors had bought the two storey property and renovated it into the most ideal flats. Two flats to be precise. The top flat had been already sold on to an elderly couple, and the bottom flat was now ready for sale and I was determined it would be ours. So determined in fact, that I haunted our solicitor daily and tortured him into finding me what the top offer on the flat was. I knew this was wrong of me, but it was the only way I had of getting the house. As, in Scotland, the top offer purchases the property. Therefore, to say I went out of my way to find the top offer, would be mild. When eventually against all odds, I found out the top offer, whereby, by extending our already tightly stretched mortgage, I promptly topped it again and succeeded in the purchase of our "Dream Home" not knowing, a dream home, nightmares were made of.

Big changes were in store for me I felt. I changed my job also, at that time, to a very responsible post as receptionist for a TV rental company and could still manage to keep up my façade for long enough in my new job. As I was responsible for the cash; responsible for the stock, and even was a key holder, responsible for the whole outfit. Except, I'm an alcoholic, and was never ever responsible for myself. The first and worst disaster struck on the day we were to move to our new home. My Granny died and inwardly so did I. To me, my world ended that day. I always knew, by law of nature my beloved Granny would probably die before I did, but I also always knew I would never be able to cope or accept her death. I truly loved her with a passion indescribable. She was everything to me, all my life, she was my mother, father, grandmother, guardian and best friend. How in under God could I go on now without her? To say I was devastated is an understatement. I felt gutted, numb, and horrifically orphaned and alone. I had only left her the day before, happy and cheery, rosy cheeked and glowing. She left me to the door of her flat and waved with me yelling happily "I'll see you tomorrow Mum" and now, tomorrow was horrifically today, and she is dead. I knew I'd never live without her and I had no intention of doing so. A despair, a desperate depression and deep sorrow set in instantly on me, and I wanted to die with her. I swear to God, my reader, I truly wanted to die. My Granny had only ever feared one thing in her strict God fearing life, and that was death. She had an enormous fear of dying and would pray constantly to "Go in her sleep." Everyday I used to ask her "What are you praying for so constantly?" and she would answer "Well Marilyn, my prayers have already been answered, to see me spared to see you reared and happy, and I just pray everyday in thanks, and also, when my time comes, to go in my sleep." And once more, today, her prayers had been answered. For that my dear reader, is just how it happened, she'd gone to bed that night before and simply died in her sleep. But although my Granny's prayers had been answered, it still left me; now in tatters, alcoholic, suicidal, with a sorrow beyond belief, engulfing me like a shroud. Nothing mattered now, like emptiness in my heart was unbearable pain. I was lost, alone in a dark sad world of my own, without my Granny in it. I was now in a hell of sadness and unspeakable despair, and believe me, reader, if I drank before, I lost her, by God, my drinking hadn't really started at all, until now. I didn't care a jot for anything, anybody or any consequences. The thought of living life without my Granny was a living death. I sought complete oblivion from bottle after bottle of vodka, but I could not even achieve this. For all I drank, I could not even pass out, never mind pass away. My special bond as I called it, had gone, I only ever had that special bond with my Granny, and I remember distinctly telling everyone this, including my mother, through drunken tears, as my Granny's body lay in her coffin for three days, in the very room she and I shared for most of my life. I was a complete disgrace at her funeral. I had been in the corpse room with a bottle in my hand, actually lifting my Granny's head from her coffin pillow. Pleading with her not to leave me, swigging down vodka between sobs. Pleading with the woman, who taught me "Drink was a curse" and here was I now, with not even the respect to leave the bottle down to bury her. I am ashamed to this day at my drunken behaviour at my Granny's funeral. I was so very drunk at the funeral Mass, I had to be carried out of the church and left once more on the street. I did not want to be sober, even my mother managed to stay sober that day, but not me. For yes, drink was a curse, for it surely cursed me.

Still, life is so strange and unpredictable that through all the horror and sadness I remember two darkly comical incidents that happened at the time. The first being, on the evening my

Granny's coffin went into the chapel to lay overnight until the morning after, when the actual funeral Mass service and burial would take place.

We all filed into the church together for the short evening service with confession included for those who desired this. I remember as my mother had for years and years neglected her religious duties, I pleaded and begged her, for my Granny to rest in peace, to please, go back to confession that evening if only to allow her to receive communion at my Granny's funeral Mass. "No way" my mother screamed, "Its years since I went to confession". "It would take me a month to list my sins, and another month to confess them and anyhow, I don't want a lecture from strict Father Maloney either." "Please go in" I urged, "Please, Please Tricia, You'll feel better for confessing especially after all these years". "I'll see" she reluctantly answered.

Anyhow, I remember my good living wee mother in law telling me to "Leave my mother be, to make her own mind up". Well, as my mother in law was nearly as holy as my Granny, with mass every day and prayers abound, I thought then I would take her wise advice and leave my mother to decide for herself. Only I could not leave her be, for I thought on another idea to help her confess. As we filed into the church, my in-laws all sat in the Pugh in front of us, as we all awaited confession to start, and my mother would be second. I had now managed to persuaded her eventually to "go in" after me. Anyhow, as I went into the confessional first, I started to tell the strict father about my mother who was about to come in next. I drunkenly told him "She's not been to Mass for years and years". "Not been to confession since the 1960's, has led a drunken life, and a child out of wed-lock" and on and on and on I ranted to the Priest.

"Remember to give her a good talking to Father. I'll send her in now." "Yes, you do that my child" Father Maloney said sternly, "Send her in now." His strict authority reminding me of my beloved Granny.

As I left the confession box, I tapped my mothers shoulder whispering "In you go now" shaking and fearful, with beads of cold seat sprouting on her forehead, she rose to go into the small confession box, only to turn back on her heels, tap my wee holy mother in law on the shoulder. She said to her "You go in Maggie before me, I feel I need more time to think of my sins." As I stood aghast, my mother said to me "It's alright Marilyn, I promise I will go in next, when Wee Maggie comes out." Well, panic set in me, as my good living mother in law was detained in the confession box for what seemed like forever, presumably, getting all sorts of ranting and raving on the road to righteousness from Father Maloney and with her never far from the alter rails. She eventually emerged from the confession box, ashen faced and very shocked and shaky looking. "Good God" my mother whispered to me, "Wee Maggie must have had a lot worse to tell him than me, I'll go in now, I feel better. I know I wont need half the time Wee Maggie took" she gleed.

The second incident was on the evening of my Granny's funeral after the burial. As a family, we all wanted to go back to my Granny's flat to sit together without any interruptions whatsoever. Our friends and neighbours respected this, and we returned home with just six of us being, my Aunt Cathie, her man, my Uncle John, my Uncle Duncan, my mother, Tommy and myself. We sat in a sort of circle crying, chatting, even laughing at some of my Granny's antics throughout her long colourful life. With being such a superstitious family, I then said "You can actually feel mums presence in the house, as if she not gone at all!" And as you can imagine it was quite an eerie feeling, as all her belongings, her beloved holy pictures were all around us. "Let's make tea" my Aunt Cathie suggested. Then my mother decided she had best start on her long journey home to Paisley. "I'll run you home" said my Uncle John. Poor Uncle

John had suffered years with his chronic asthma. "Are you sure?" said my mother. "Yes, of course" said Uncle John. "Stay a while longer." We did this, and chatted more and more about my beloved departed Granny.

As pubs were now emptying in the area for closing time we realised the chosen few "drunken pests" would now be knocking our door looking for funeral drink or excuses to drink to my Granny's sad departure. My Granny specifically did not wish for alcohol to be taken, especially at her funeral. So, on hearing the street below becoming noisy and rowdy with party revellers, my mother decided that, when she and Uncle John left, we would put out our main lights, as the street light would be sufficient, and therefore, any drunks would think on seeing our house in darkness, to move on. We agreed to this, and I promptly left my mother and Uncle John to the door, wishing them a safe journey. I walked the long dark hallway, back to the dark living room to join the remainder of the family. We now sat in a sort of small circle in darkness, with the bright street light shinning in the window. It all felt even more eerie than before twenty minutes past and we were still chatting about how you could actually "feel" my granny's presence in the flat. "It's almost as though she hasn't gone" my Uncle Duncan said. When then, heavy footsteps came down the long hallway and stopped directly at the living room door. We were stunned and frightened as we all stared at each other, with the street light. All we could see were the terrified whites of our eyes, glowing in the near darkness, when a heavy hand went onto the door handle and the door very slowly creaked open. We were numb to our seats in fear. My Granny had returned? A white-haired head then came around the door in the darkness "Only me" cried my Uncle John. "I've forgotten my inhaler" and returned to fetch it. "I wouldn't want to take an asthma turn on the journey folks." Well reader, if anyone were going to take a turn it was Cathie, Duncan, Tommy and me with sheer fright, thinking we had summoned up my Granny's spirit from the grave already. Needless to say, I for one, sobered up instantly that night. My Granny would have been looking down on us having a great chuckle to herself.

My pleasure and excitement had now totally gone completely from the purchase of my new home. In fact, I remember on the day of the 'flitting' I sat all day long just drinking and drinking, one vodka after the other, whilst removal men worked and scurried around me with no clue to the sad numb world I was in. I recall they lifted the fridge and the food fell out onto the floor, and as they lifted the washing machine out, from the kitchen unit, the washing actually fell out also, onto the floor. I was so drunk and disinterested to care. "Come and sit with me fellows and have drink" I slurred. "Ehh, no thanks Missus we're working" they replied. "Huh" I remember grunting "How could two big lumps of men refuse a free drink from me?" What was wrong with them I thought? But I know today, they were not like me, they did not want nor need a drink at two o'clock in the afternoon. They were not alcoholics so what was wrong with me, quite simply I was an alcoholic.

My new home held no happy feelings whatsoever, but I blamed that on my grief and sorrow at losing my beloved Granny. There was a constant coldness throughout the house, which no amount of heating nor fires could change the atmosphere. One room in particular I could not heat. I swear every heater I put in that room made no difference whatsoever. Even when my mother purchased a new calor gas heater as a welcome in gift for us. It blew up, the moment I lit it. I could never heat the house at all. And with me being so superstitious I always felt so uneasy and unwelcome in the house. From the very first day I entered it. My saving grace were my lovely old neighbours who lived in the flat directly above. And with only two flats in the property it was a delight to know John and Betty were to be our neighbours. They were truly lovely people and I recall on our first introduction I returned to their flat immediately with a bottle of whiskey for John and chocolates and flowers for Betty. John reassuring me, "Never, to worry or fear living below, as they would always be there to call on, for any reason whatsoever to help day or night." This made me feel so very safe at least; as Tommy worked long distance driving and was gone overnight on many many occasions with his work. I was alone.

As we lived near to what was considered a bad end of town, with gangs, coming down from the housing schemes directly behind us. I had many sleepless nights of worry, as a particularly group of unsavoury boys, would congregate nightly in a gang, just directly on the corner our house lay. If I were alone in the evening, I would often call up to John and Betty for an hours chat and always, would they kindly reassure me that I could rely on them at any time. I remember thinking how fortunate I was to have them as my neighbours and I would always just thank them with a little token each week of flowers for Betty, and, Tommy would leave for overnight journeys, happy enough knowing our neighbours were such good and reliable people.

Although I drank alcoholically I could never actually get what I called drunk, I was only constantly in a sort of topped up numbness. Now, I was not getting any of the things I used to think I drank for my drinking had a very odd opposite effect on my actual intentions now. For instance, I would sit all night and drink to be happy, and became unhappy. I would drink to seek joy and become morbidly sad instead. I would drink to make friends, and I made many enemies. I would drink to be life and soul, and became obnoxious. I would drink to fix problems, and I'd only watch them multiply. I would drink to cope with life, but little did I know I was inviting death.

There was also another cursed eyesore directly outside my

front door, and that was a local bus stop. Over the previous years when our building had lay derelict, people would shelter in the porch of the house from rain, whilst awaiting buses. This now, was still happening with people coming right into my porch and hallway to shelter. I remember at the end of my tether rushing out one particular evening as I chased the queue of passengers away from my front door. I threw a large black plastic bin bag over the bus stop and tied it tightly with the approaching bus driver shouting and swearing at me for my actions. In return, I gave him as good as I got in retaliation. Eventually though, with much crying to the local district council, the bus stop moved to a more appropriate area, on up the road and a shelter for the people to stand in. "Oh God, weren't people hateful" I'd cry. Especially since my Granny's death I hated everything and everyone. But more so, I hated myself. What I had become was never my beloved Granny's intentions for me. For all her prayers for me to turn out well, I turned out so very very bad, evil in fact. I now felt evil, the more I drank the more badness would come into my head. I was now so obsessed with the supernatural. I would drink the clock round all night long. I would conjure up my long lost Granny, chatting away to her quite naturally, with Tommy coming into the room, wondering if I had neighbours in the house. "Who are you chatting to?" he'd say. "Get out, go away" I'd squeal at him. "You wouldn't ever understand, leave me alone" I'd cry. I'm sure with my madness and alcoholism he was so glad to have overnight long distance trips to get away from me. And so was I, for I could not stand his 'nagging me' either. Three months after we moved into our new home it started, the broken windows. At least once every two weeks, we would come home to find yet another window in the house broken deliberately with bricks and stones. I would be terrified when Tommy would have to go to work and I was alone. At any time a stone or brick would come hurling through a window,

and we could never find any evidence of who was to blame.
I recall the first time it happened and I was alone in the
house, I ran up to John and Betty's flat crying, with John
telling me "Calm down Marilyn, we will find the culprits."
John was so certain it was two rough boys from the corner
gang nicknamed 'Wee Simba' and 'Big Murdie'.
I only new 'Wee Simba' and 'Big Murdie' to see, and that
was enough. They did continually hang around in the bad
looking gang from the area. So yes, it could well be them.
As they knew we did not want them congregating around our
house, so John promised to keep an eye on my house,
although he was very deaf he could see what was going on. I
thanked him so very much, handing Betty a large box of
chocolates for their trouble. We got a small wall built around
the house, but I remember on returning home from work that
same evening. The wall was viciously attacked with the
graffiti written on the soft cement and horrific slogans
wrecking the builders work. The rear garden fence of the
house was continually kicked in every other day, with empty
alcohol bottles and cans strewn throughout the garden area
most mornings. I was demented with fear and worry. Police
could not detect the culprits nor could we. Until one evening
after yet once more, a brick came through the kitchen
window. John came rushing down to tell us "I seen them
Marilyn, I told you 'Wee Simba and 'Big Murdie', they are
your culprits." "Oh, thank you John" Tommy and I gushed.
Not only the fear of living there, but the cost of double
glazing on a constant basis was infuriating. Tommy once
more reached for his jacket to go out to tackle the boys, and
sure enough, they were all in the gang on the corner directly
outside our house. "Wait Tommy" I cried, "there's too many
of them, don't go out tackling them in anger. Listen, I've an
idea, why don't you get friendly with them instead?"
"What?" said Tommy. "You'll be wanting me to join the
gang next" he exclaimed. "I know what I'll do with them" he

answered. "No, please get friendly instead" I said, "For we still don't have the proof to blame them". "Oh well, OK" Tommy reluctantly grumbled. As I watched cautiously from the kitchen window, I realised Tommy was indeed using a different approach to the gang. On slightly opening my kitchen window, I could now hear the conversation taking place. Tommy singled out the two leaders, 'Wee Simba' and 'Big Murdie' and very civilly asked them "Listen boys, someone is continually breaking our windows. Do you know anything about it?" 'Big Murdie' rushed to their defence, "Are you trying to say its us?" He growled, "No, no" exclaimed Tommy nervously "but I want to ask your help boys" Tommy continued in his new friendly approach. "If you see or hear of anyone smashing the glass, will you please let us know?"

Simba and Murdie backed down, we were actually appearing to put our trust in them. My tactic was working. "Aye, sure thing" Murdie scowled. "But let me say Tommy, if we find out who it is they're dead." Oh, my I hadn't planned on taking it that far but at least we had the gang more on our side now, even although we still had their guilt in doubt. Our vandalism nightmares still continued for many months to follow. So afraid was I, that I actually kept a hammer below my bed, for as the windows were ground level, I really never knew the minute I could easily be attacked. For there was nothing to stop the perpetrator not only smashing the windows but stepping in the actual house at the same time was my greatest fear. The nightmares continued on, until one evening eventually the whole thing came to a horrific end.

That evening, Tommy and I had been out trying to celebrate our wedding anniversary, when about 11 pm on returning home, Tommy decided he would walk up the road to the fish and chip shop for a carry out supper. I was reluctant for him to venture into the bad area at that time of night. "I'll be ok" Tommy urged. "I'll only be gone a short time. By the time you've boiled the kettle for tea, I'll be back" he reassured me. "What about the gangs" I urged, "They gather at the chip shop corner. Don't go" I pleaded. "Look Marilyn, I will be fine" he insisted, as he closed the back door behind him.

I worried just the same and I hurriedly went into wash my hands in our big empty bathroom. Suddenly through the closed venetion blinds the bathroom window was being viciously smashed in, with some sort of large pole. I started to scream hysterically when just then, someone was banging on our kitchen back door, shouting "Marilyn, it's John from upstairs, I've just seen who done it, open the door". "Are you alright?"

As I nervously opened the door, I was relieved to fall into old Johns arms. Thank God for him. "Marilyn, I was right all along, I saw them myself" he screamed, "It was Wee Simba and Big Murdie from the gang. They smashed your windows in with that clothes pole. They are the culprits" he screeched. Just then from out of nowhere, appeared Tommy walking down the road Wee Simba and Big Murdie accompanying him from the chip shop. They had been nowhere near my house. The culprit was in fact unbelievably yes, my great old neighbour, John.

At hearing themselves being wrongly accused Simba and Murdie instantly leap on old John and as Murdie had a hold on him by the throat, I was crying "Let him go, he's old. He has a bad heart condition." By now John was turning purple, losing his breath, with Murdies hands around his neck, trying to squeeze the life out of him. Eventually Murdie let John go from his grasp. "You auld bastard" Murdie screamed at John. "You let us take the fucking blame for months and all the time it was you. I'll fucking kill you." Murdie cried again. By now I had rang for the police who appeared and promptly charged John for the crimes. We took John to court and he was charged and found guilty, but because of his age, he was not jailed but was summoned to pay the backload of costs to us and he also was given a very heavy fine for his actions of vandalism and harassment over the long period to us.

I could not believe this 'lovely' neighbour couple could do this to me, but their motives became clear, when Johns daughter called in on us to 'apologise' for her fathers actions. It so happened when we were purchasing the flat, so also, was John's daughter, and if you remember reader, I told you previously that we "topped" the top offer well, that top offer was indeed John's daughters own offer on the flat. This angered John and Betty so much, that we had gazumped their daughter on the purchase, they then, in turn, decided to make our life a misery. They tried in vain to force us out of the flat. "How could I be so stupid Tommy" I said unbelievably "I was such a fool to continually thank them for watching our house, when all the time they were not only wrecking our property, but our lives too." Needless to say, we left that flat, and gladly sold it on to new buyers, whom I felt would need a lot of luck to say the least. No, need I add did I sell it to John's daughter who actually had the audacity and nerve to put in an offer once more. No, this time I would accept the lowest offer rather than sell her the flat for what her parents put us through was not only unbelievable, but unforgivable too. I distinctly remember as I signed a welcome home card to the new buyers writing 'Good Luck in your new home' and thinking to myself with neighbours from hell like John and Betty, they'd need a bit more than Good Luck. We moved once more. This time with luck seeming to smile on us. We bought a lovely modern detached house right in amongst the 'West End' of town, 'The posh area'. My neighbours were now monied people, doctors, lawyers, and the like. I was now in among the gentry of the town, the toffee nosed and the Ok-yah's. The true fact being I had managed to get the house at a knockdown price, otherwise I could never have afforded the area. But one thing in life I have no time for, are 'snobs' and now I was truly in amongst them in the west-end and they did not know what had hit them, for I now had an even more hardened attitude, after trusting my previous 'lovely neighbours'. There was no way on this earth, I would ever be bullied again by neighbours. No, I would do my own thing this time, west-end or not, no one would ever be allowed to 'dictate' to me again in my own home. No, this time I'd call the shots, drink when I wanted, party when I wanted, summon up the devil himself if I wanted and that's just what I did. No this time there would definitely be 'No Half Measures'.

My drinking had now escalated rapidly, if that were possible, knowing the stage of alcoholism I was already at. But I know today, alcohol is cunning, powerful and baffling and can only progress worse for the suffering alcoholic. It truly never gets better. My whole world centred around alcohol, how to get it, the means to buy it, where to hide it, the thought of having 'no' drink in the house literally paralysed me with fear. By now with my convincing sick brain twisted with drink, I did not even need money to stay drunk. Tommy would lock me in my room, and I'd get out. He would lock me out of the house, and I'd get in. My work suffered drastically. I would be on my knees of a morning with a bottle in my hand, vomiting and sweating, head down the toilet bowl praying, yes praying to God to keep the first drink down. I'd swallow the alcohol and it would automatically spew back up like the River Shannon from my stomach and it would be swallowed back down. Up, down, up, down, until I would get the first drink down. Sweat, bile, vomit dripping off my face, my poor husband would stand at the toilet door and cry "Don't drink today, please don't drink today Marilyn." I'd turn and very impolitely tell him where to go.

This performance would be daily, before I could even think of dressing myself for to face work. I simply had to have that first drink to feel remotely 'normal'. Then the full palava from my medicine cabinet, paracetamol, aspirin, alka-seltzer, digest, polo mints, perfume, make-up, disguise, hiding, camouflage, nothing had changed only it got more and more drastic and tragic. I'd waltz into the pub in my 'liquid lunch hour' and have not a penny in my possession, and I'd loudly announce to my drinking cronies "This is my birthday," and swiftly there would be my usual magic words spat at me. "What are you having Marilyn?" and with my birthday being six months past, I'd quite happily drink my hour away for free, with not an ounce of guilt, then tomorrow, in another drinking hole, "This is my anniversary" I'd cry. "What are you having Marilyn?" This convincing was just part and parcel of my drinking addiction. I am not proud of my behaviour, reader, but I was a very very sick person and alcohol, and how to get it was my one and only priority. My flyness would work on overdrive hand in glove with my chronic alcohol addiction, I was a fiend, a sick fiend, I was so also totally obsessed with the occult. I was like a woman possessed. Reading palms of women around all the pubs, never ever, may I add, for money, but for drink only. So long as a gaggle of women would ply me with drink all night long, then I'd read their hands all night long, and believe it or not reader, the drunker I got, the better I became at the readings. It was truly as if the more "Devils Brew" I consumed the more evil I became. In a strange way, my accuracy at fortune telling was very well known, and I was never short of eager clients awaiting readings. In also my desperation though, never would I allow cash to change hands only drink.

I remember distinctly on one sunny afternoon, when I was half drunk and feeling anything but sunny, the front door was being knocked. As I shakily opened the door, I was rather shell shocked to see my local Priest confronting me. Keeping him at the doorway I drunkenly mumbled, "Hello Father, how can I help you?" Dear God, little did I know it should have been the other way around. It was me who needed help. "Marilyn" the Priest gushed, "It's come to my attention that you're doing the work of the devil! Palmistry, reading hands around pubs" he said. "Is this true?" he continued. I stared at him obnoxiously and slurred "Why, what's your problem father?" "Are you afraid you missed your place in the queue?" I said with venom in my sick reply cheeky and cocky I continued on angrily. "Come in now and I'll fix you in for a quick reading, no charge just say a prayer for me." Evil rising in me, I knew my beloved Granny would turn in her grave to hear me talk to the Priest like this. Nothing frightened me, no one frightened me. I could be fine enough one minute in the pub, then any moment later, I would be violent and uncontrollable, unpredictable and I'm sure very frightenly mad.

Getting drunk was not a problem for me now, but keeping it down in my stomach was. I would vomit day and night, I got so obnoxious and awful that I would not even attempt to remove myself from the barstool to the toilet, and would just vomit all down my front where I sat, just wiping my mouth to gulp yet another mouthful of alcohol down. I was in and out of hospitals now, on a continual basis. Jaundiced yellow, eyes like egg yolks, face like a big banana, signing myself out of hospital, was a well know trait of mine. How the wonderful doctors and nurses put up with me I shall never know. "You won't see thirty Marilyn" the specialist told me on my twenty eighth birthday. "Good" I crowed, in my cock of the north attitude "At least I'll go merrily, with a glass in my hand" I spat back at him cheek and venom pouring from my every word. Feeling truly in my sad sick heart reader that twenty eight was long enough to live like this, I did not even wish to face twenty nine, for by now I was already dead.

By some fluke miracle, I still half-managed to keep my day job, but gone was the glamour, now I'd get the barber to shave my head, as I could not be bothered fafing around with hair of any description either my own, or otherwise. I'd plaster on my mask of wax camouflage but any glamour now had long gone. I'd get through my days only just, with the thought of my cargo of drink. The only thing allowing me to do so, were thoughts of my drunken weekend ahead with my mother, somehow, spurred me on in the long week.

My mother by now was in her own hellish drunken world. We were not wanted anymore, anywhere for our music and song. And now we were reduced to weekends playing in the biggest dives in Paisley, where the few drunken customers were very much like ourselves. In a dark haze of drink, sawdust, and spittoons. We didn't care how we sounded, for nobody really listened. Fights would break out. Police would be called and very often I would be the instigator. My mother and I would stagger home to her bare house, armed with plastic bags full of drink, but not much to sit on. My mother had nothing left. Jaws had even left her now, for that much I was glad of. But she was very much in her own alcoholic hell. Jaws took her furniture, even her very refrigerator. For that, I'll never forgive him but at least my brother Wee Jim stuck with her through out everything.

Wee Jim was now six foot tall, and becoming very much his own man. He would never complain to us for our drunken lives, but it really hit home to me when one night, I nagged him as usual to "take a drink Jim, come on you boring tea-total" I'd scorn "A good drink is what you are missing" I'd cry, forcing him wishing for him to "Join in" our drunken sessions. When on one evening he exploded in anger in my face, and told me straight. "Marilyn, leave me alone". "I don't drink for I see my father, my mother and you drunk and thats enough to keep me sober!" I never once forced him to drink ever again.

My day job supplied me with a nice company outfit consisting of skirt, matching jacket and waist coat, so I didn't even have to worry about dressing myself now either. I could wear my three piece suit day and night. And that just what I did. I'd go straight from my job, to the pubs at 5.30 p.m. and

God knows how or when I would get home. Only for the care and unbelievable love of Tommy, searching for me in pubs helping me home whilst getting a vile mouthful of abuse from me. He truly was a saint to say the least for what he had to put with, I could never fill a hundred books.

One particular morning, I woke up lying in my hallway from where presumably I fell, the night before. As I came sickly around, I realised I was missing half of my good three piece suit my company had supplied me. I now really panicked scrambling around looking for the remainder of my outfit, as I only had the skirt and blouse, I was still wearing, where in under God was the jacket and waist coat? Well, it did not take me long to find out reader, as my front door knocked loudly. I frighteningly slowly opened it, to see to my horror, one of my posh neighbours, the doctor's wife actually standing before me with my jacket and waistcoat dangling from her forefinger. With her nose in the air she pounced "I believe these are yours?" "Oh my" I stuttered, "Your name badge is on the label" she snobly slurred. "I found your clothes lying on my lawn this morning" she continued haughtily. "I'm sorry" I squeaked, "they must have blew off my washing line during the night and into your garden" I lied. "No" she squealed, "You were drunkenly rolling around in my garden during the night, singing and squealing at the top of your voice and let me say if it happens again I'll jail you". "In my opinion," she continued in her snobby attitude, "You have a very sever problem and you need help. You're an alcoholic my dear." Well, like a red rag to a bull, "You fuck off ya snobby auld bastard". "Don't you call me an alcoholic" I screeched. "I've seen you in Tesco's with your big cargo of dinner wines" I slurred. "Twitching curtains, swigging away at the wine yourself. Only thing is" I cried, "I do it in the open and you swally in the dark". "Now you get off my lawn" I cried, and I slammed the door in her face.

God! I hated snobs, hypocrites, pots calling the kettles black.

That's all I was surrounded by in this west end no wonder I drink I mumbled to myself. All these Hooray-hendrys looking down on me, never out of the golf club, never played a round of golf in their lives, only ordering a round of drinks in the nineteenth hole, telling me I've a problem Huh. They're my only problem around here. If only that were so, my dear reader. If only they were my only problem I would have been quite fine but no, I knew deep in my heart, my neighbour was right. I did have a problem, a big problem and seeing her so called faults, had only temporarily justified me now.

To carry on, giving you a catalogue of my drunken horrors, would, my reader take many many books to fill but suffice to say, as the days crept slowly and painfully on and on I knew, yes I knew I had to do something about my addiction. For now, I was hurting bad. I was sore I was in agony mentally, physically and spiritually dead. To die at this stage would have been a blessed release and going straight to hell, would have been a party to the hell I was in on earth. Mentally I was off my head, a mad woman constantly topped up with drink, thinking drink, planning how to get drink, hiding drink, worse, forgetting where I hid drink, panic struck pulling out cupboards and drawers searching for drink. Hiding in alley ways and closes guzzling drink thinking I was invisible to the public. Changing pubs and off licence explaining to assistants the drink was for my visitors. Lies, lies, lies. As if anyone cared. Everyone knew the drink was for me. Yes! I was mental alright. Did things a sane person would not have considered doing. Did things I would never consider doing in my sober life years ago, which now seemed to belong to another life. Not mine, for I had now been drunk more years than I had lived sober, and physically sick, well say no more, my body was by now very very close to shut down. The pain in my stomach, liver and fierce palpitating thudding in my heart was unbearable. Constant vomiting black blood, green bile and sweat dripping from every pore in my body was now unbearable. Every day the same scenario, the same pattern of horror and pain. This was not what I took drink for this was not want I called "enjoying myself". Why had it come to this? I loved a sing-song and a party and a fun time. This was not a party now. This was anything but fun, and spiritually I was dead. God? What God? I would use him alright, like Santa Clause. God get me, God give me, all me, me, me, my way or no way. Constantly torturing, pleading, bargaining with this Santa God and if he didn't do for me what I asked he didn't exist. No, reader, my God would not surely see one of his flock sink to hell before his very eyes. There must be no God at all.

My so called spiritual feelings had all gone in the wrong direction towards hell with my black thoughts moods and desires. I was sick, sick and dying. At thirty one years old, one year older than the specialists had predicated my lifespan. They couldn't even get that right or I would have been gone from my hell a year ago, and at least I would have been out of it all. That would have been a blessing compared to trying to live in it. I do not say this lightly my reader, my desire to die was overwhelming by now, for I had no desire to continue to live like this anymore. Dying would have been so much easier now than the thought of stopping drinking. That thought to me was a sheer impossibility.

My failed attempts at suicide were due to my faithful husband Tommy getting me to hospitals once more to be patched up. Papered over the cracks. No, something else had to be done for me. But what? I was mentally, physically, and spiritually beat. No will of my own, no soul, had no heart left in me. I was beat. But still, I defended my drink to the end. People were right I was a hopeless case, who just would or could not stop drinking. I knew in my poor sick head cutting down was not an option. But stopping was an absolute no no. Nothing short of a miracle could or would get me to stop. Nothing. So death was my only other solution in my mind. This time, I'd do the job right. This time yes, I'd get it done properly. This time, there would defiantly be 'No Half Measures'.

I was to carry on drinking for yet another month, when one evening whilst sitting drinking and listening to my mother gibber and chat drunkenly at me, I suddenly put my bottle down and said to her "We need help, we need help" I cried. "Look at me, look at you, mother and daughter, not even a seat to sit on, a pot to piss in and yet surrounded by drink and empty bottles we need help" I screamed. "Shut up, shut up" she shouted at me, "You're depressing me, shut up, shut up and drink up".

And I did just that. I shut up and I continued to drink up. But I knew something would need to be done for me, whether my mother agreed or not. But what? One more month on I was to have big party, for Alan was coming home on a visit, remember Alan was one of the two deserted children my granny had reared. I bucked myself up a bit for his return, and miraculously planned his welcome home party. Even planned the party around my day off my day job. So I could really let myself go and do my own thing at the party, without the thought of work the next day glowering over me.

Another year was ending, and I wondered vaguely what 1985 would hold in store for me. Little did I know 1985 came around with nothing new to me, still in my drunken world, dark world, sad world, my special welcome party for Alan Rose was miraculously planned more for me than him, but nevertheless, on the day preceding my big do, my manager at work pleaded with me to come in to work the day following my party, as due to illness, they were short staffed, and really I was a last resort. As I had well pre-planned this as my day off, I was truly panicked at this request, and rather then eagerly agree to come into work and be a faithful servant to my job. I had to think of the drunken, sick hung-over state

I'd be in that day as I was after all, only a faithful servant to the bottle. "I'll come into work, if I must" but deep down dreading the very thought.

The party came around. Alan came from USA to visit, all went well that evening. No fights, no police, just a good happy party for his homecoming. All the guests left eventually, leaving Alan and I sitting chatting and drinking on. My husband had long retired to bed warning and nagging me it was two am. "Oh, let Tommy go to his bed Alan" I chirped, "He's such a wet blanket, sure I never see you and we have so much to catch up on." Drink after drink got poured and drank mainly by me, laughing, playing music, reminising, crying with Alan over the loss of my Granny. After all, she was his Granny too. Time flew on, and on until Alan stopped me in my drunken tracks, telling me it was six am. I was after all having to go to work at nine. "Oh, don't you worry Alan" I slurred, "It's a doddle". "I always go to work, straight from the party. No problem to me". "Another coat of emulsion over the face, and I'm fine". "Drink up."

Ten minutes to nine appeared, and as I crawled to the bathroom mirror after vomiting into the sink, I drunkenly stared at myself in the mirror, slapping a coat of pan stick over my swollen haggard face. I was actually wishing I had listened to Tommy's nagging, back at 2 am. I got into my work "late" as usual with my Manager and colleagues speechless at the sight of me. "Oh look at their sad old faces" I thought. "Cheer up you lot" I squealed, "It's a new year, chill out a bit" I gibbered. As I know today, my manager was just too shocked and frightened to attempt to send me home. Just stared at me as I flopped down at my desk in the shop floor ready to meet my public.

Customers came and went, with me giggling and chatting like a budgie, with not a drunken care to their needs. Eleven am came around and Alan-Rose appeared in the shop to thank me for the party and bid me farewell till next time. Lunches did not start until one pm but I grabbed my coat, and told my boss I was "Going for my dinner, C'mon Alan, I'll take you to Tokyo Joes Pub for a liquid farewell lunch, and you'll meet my cronies there too." Alan looked disturbed and asked if that was alright to walk out of my job. "Oh, don't mind that sad lot Alan" I chirped, "They're just jealous they're stuck there all day."

I proceeded to swallow back my liquid lunch merrily and had yet another little cry on saying goodbye to Alan. Then reluctantly tramped my way back to work at 1 pm. The Staff took another shocked look at me, as I pranced into the back shop to hang up my coat. "God, such faces on this sad crowd I work with," I was mumbling out loud. "A good drink would kill them" I stammered. Just then, the Assistant Manageress appeared from her lunch break, clutching a gift wrapped bottle of Martini to take visiting that evening to her friend's house, but when she had a customer, I opened her Martini, and drank it. I shall never ever forget her face as she came back into the staff room. Chin dropped to her chest, eyes bulging from their sockets "I don't believe this" she shrieked, "I just don't believe what I'm seeing" she squealed "You're an alcoholic a chronic alcoholic, does it ever end with you" she cried. "Oh, what's your problem?" I cockily said putting the bottle back to my lips to drain it. "Do you want a wee drink too?" I slurred "Get a cup and I'll pour you one" I chuckled. "I don't want you to feel left out, that would never do." She just stood dumbstruck with me as I proceeded to drink her drink or rather, what was left of her drink.

From the back shop, I could see out to the front shop, when just then a snobby customer came in and I jumped forward saying "I'll serve her." I had been serving this high and mighty woman for nine years every month, as she paid for her rental television. I always knew she "looked down" on me, like something she stepped on and yes, I'd serve her alright.

With my body physically in the shop, my head and heart were definitely back in the pub, and God, did I hate snobs. "Hello, there Madam" I slurred "Can I help you?" "Yes" she carefully mumbled in her snooty accent. "I'll have two video tapes." "Oh, really", I replied, "No you wont you'll have four video tapes" I demanded. "Don't make that cheque out for two, for I'm not selling you two. Your getting four" I cackled.

"Your drunk" she snapped, "Aye" I agreed "And you're a pain in the arse, and I have been dying to tell you that for nine years" and I got sacked immediately. I was hauled out of the shop on my hands and knees and thrown once more onto the street with people walking and tramping over me. "Does a condemned woman not get a last phone call" I cried in the shop door. "I have to phone Tommy to come for me, please" I begged. The manager trailed me back into the back shop reluctantly and allowed me to telephone my husband. "Come and get me" I slurred to Tommy on the phone. "They're throwing me out of here" and with that, the management promptly flung me out of the backdoor onto my knees. I lay there on the ground until Tommy pulled up beside me and lifted me into the car away from the dustbins surrounding me.

"Nine years" I cried "Nine years with that company and that's what they do to me. Get me home, get me home now" I shrieked. Tommy just looked so sad and low and shook his head, and for once did not give out to me. But instead, he started up the car and repeating over and over "I've had it, I've had enough. I've just had it this time with you." "Oh, shut up" I ranted, "get me home now."

I had had five full bottles of vodka hidden through the house but, as I had the taste of Martini I headed straight for Tommy's special dinner wine rack and proceeded to poke the cork of his favourite "guest wine" in with a fork and I started now to drink it and guzzle it down immediately. "Are you never going to fucking stop" he screamed shaking me by the shoulders. I then picked up my serrated bread knife from the kitchen worktop and slashed once more into my wrists squealing, shouting and crying blood flying everywhere. I never did cut bread with that knife just arms. "I want to die, I want to die" I screeched. "You don't know what its like, I want to die." "Oh shut up, shut up" Tommy cried, "Do it right, do it right this time". "Listen" he cried as he shook me by the shoulders, "Listen, I want to die, I want to die and don't drink. I want to die living with you. Now do it right!"

He wants to die I'd never thought of him before having to live with me and my mother. Oh my God no wonder he wants to die. This stuck miraculously in my brain. I had no idea and gave absolutely no thought of his suffering only me, me, me.

"I'm off" he shouted, "I'm gone this time for good" he cried. "I'll be back only for my things when you not here" he shouted. "I can't and won't take living with you another day. You're a chronic drunk and I hate you for what you've become and taken me right down with you." "Go to hell" I squealed "and don't come back." But as he slammed the outside door, behind him, I knew he was gone for good this time. I knew I was a hopeless case. I knew Tommy was right. I knew I should now "do it right, for my dear reader, to die that day was in my sad brain, the only release for my drinking.

To die, was much easier to do that day than to give up alcohol. As I picked up the bread knife once more the telephone was ringing vaguely in the background, ringing and ringing. I stared at the shiny knife with Tommy's words in my head "Do it right, Do it right". Ring, ring, ring ring the telephone rang on continually and I somehow snapped out of my suicide trance wrapped two towels around my arms and answered the phone.

It was my Aunt Cathie "You've been sacked, you're an

alcoholic, you've been dismissed from your job" she ranted on and on. "Oh, shut up" I squealed and promptly hung up on her. Alcoholic, alcoholic, alcoholic I'm so sick of people calling me that. Everybody tags me with that horrible label. I'm just a very very heavy drinker "Alcoholic" what a horrible word I mumbled to myself as blood seeped through the two thick towels I had still wrapped around my wrists. I went into my room and sat on my bed, my half bottle of wine still securely clutched in my bloodied hands. What can I do? My god what can I do? I was on a road, a dark hole of a road with no turn off. I could do what Tommy suggested for I was more than half way there. But my only alternative was to stop drinking. Oh no, oh my God no. Suicide was still the better option. As I took one more swig from my wine bottle, I happened to glance to the floor, where there lay a yellow pages telephone book, back side up with a very large advert for the Samaritans. "Do you have a problem" the black words jumped up and hit me. 'Phone the Samaritans. Talk about it now', said the wording. Then the phone number below.

I stared at the yellow book, trance like for how long I don't know even yet. Then I picked up the receiver. Beat, done, beat, king alcohol had won the battle. I was on my knees. I was mentally, physically and spiritually dead in every department of my body. I dialled the Samaritans phone number feeling still trance like that nothing anyone could say to me would or could help me. For what I had consumed alone in alcohol, I should have been dead even since yesterday. Oh yesterday, yesterday seemed another world away. The party, the constant all night drink bender, the work, the liquid lunch the Martini the work, oh my God what work I have now no job is this me at thirty one, should I live, forty one. My mother sixty one, oh my God, I was so very sick. Mixed up, and beat. I can't take it. I can't live it one more day.

"Hello" a nice calm woman's voice said "The Samaritans,

what is your problem?" "My problem" I said, "Do you have a spare couple of years to hear my problems?" Still the old cock of the north trying to come through. "I'm thirty one, I can't stop drinking my husbands left me, my mothers my drinking partner, I've lost my job, I've cut myself badly. I don't want to live. I can't live anymore. Please help me" I cried and cried. "Please help me". The woman listened silently to my pleas my ranting and raving. Then she said "Do you have drink there?" "Oh, I've drink everywhere" I replied. "Don't take another drink, and I will get you help now" the woman said in a very serious voice. "Do not take another drink, just give me your name and phone number now, and I will promise to get you help." "I'm bleeding" I cried incoherently. "The blood is dripping on the bed" I cried and managed to give the woman my name and telephone number. In hanging up, I tied the seeping wet towels tighter around my wrists, and on leaving down my wine bottle to do so, I realised I did not want another drink right then which was, a miracle alone in itself.

The phone rang and I answered it and it was a very posh woman's voice on the line, rather like the snobby voice from my dreaded shop customer. "Hello Marilyn, I'm May. I'm an alcoholic, a recovering alcoholic and I know you have a problem with drink. If you allow me, I can help you today." "Oh, please May" I cried as I continued to give her my long catalogue of horror. "Don't take another drink Marilyn, please don't take it, give me your address and I will be there directly." With the grace of God, May worked in the local hospital and arrived prepared to clean and bandage me up. I had no hair as such. I'd get the barber to shave off my hair, for I would not comb it. I was bloated two stone heavier with drink, arms bandaged up to my elbows. No care to look in any mirror to face myself. Gone was any pride, or self respect I ever had for myself. I was in hell. I was in my own self made gutter, within my very soul. I was truly beat. Alcohol had won. May tried to clean me up, and she suggested I go with her to an AA meeting. Now reader, if May had suggested, I go the edge of the pier, and jump into the River Clyde and end it, I would have said "Yes", I was truly beat alright, and I was only too willing, to follow May to anywhere or to anything on the planet, she suggested. I thank the Lord I was a very fortunate one for as I followed May, like an old rag doll, like a burnt out squib, into the AA meeting, I got the answer, and, to this day reader, I have never needed to drink again. One day at a time only, for that's all any of us have. One day, one moment, this moment in time. I know if I don't drink today, then it's always today, and by practising my teaching's I need never drink again. I firmly believe that on that very day, whilst in my own personal hell, my God, of my understanding hauled me out of that hell, by the two shoulders and said "Marilyn, you've had enough pain and you've also caused enough pain, come to believe in something higher than yourself to get sober and you will". I truly believe this happened to me, my reader, there had to be something higher than me that day, surely to God for there was truly nothing lower. Little did I know, that my life was about to change drastically by only staying away from one drink, for one day at a time, and willingly doing what the wonderful fellowship of AA suggested. Yes, my life had to change, for I was now sober and living it. It truly was a new life. Yes, two lives in one lifetime. And now I was on my wonderful voyage of discovery into my new life. And I loved that.

*My Mother, Pat Lamont at
the height of her career*

*Me, at Five Years Old
Just after my father left us.*

*My Mothers dancing school, Highland Dance Section,
I am standing far right*

My beloved Granny, my Mother, myself and my Aunt Maureen

Me, doing well with my photographic modelling in 1969

My Husband Tom (centre) "Wee Jim" and my mother

Me with my mother and pet dog "meme"

Me waiting to meet my Father in the airport for the first time in thirty one years

Me and my Father reunited

Me with my Husband Tom

*My Granny, Aunt Maureen, me, Alan and Lyn with pet dog Maxi
in my beloved Moville*

*Me with my Father enjoying
our new sober life*

Me on Holiday in Spain, Sober

Me with my beloved Grandfather whom I called 'Dad'

Part Two
My New Life

Marilyn Lamont

My excitement and enthusiasm for my new sober life was overwhelming. I did not know sobriety for 16 long painful years and I felt truly reborn. That is the only way I can describe it to my friends. I was reborn. "Change and change you must" I was taught at my regular meetings of AA and I truly tried to do everything that was suggested to me. Even although my husband returned when he saw for himself, I was, at last sober, my life was changing very nicely, but my poor mother was still alcoholically drinking. "It's a flash in the pan" she'd squeal through the telephone "Marilyn will never stay sober. It will be short lived" she'd shout very drunk herself, suffering totally with the horrific illness of alcoholism. For not only is it a lonely sad illness but it gets worse and now my mother was rapidly getting worse. Don't forget, she was seeing me in my new found wonderful sobriety but also, she had lost me as her one and only drinking partner. Sad to say my mother and I had only really got to know each other drunk. In our new life together, now, she was not coping well with the changes. She was now dreading seeing me, hiding her drink all over the house from me, in case I would "preach" sobriety to her. And I'm afraid I'd do a bit. I would tell her about AA help that was out there for her too. "No" she'd scream "that's not for me". "Leave me alone. I'm not an alcoholic. Your brainwashed" she'd shout in drink. "They have you brainwashed at that place." God help her for I surely could not. She was getting worse right in front of my eyes and I was totally helpless and hopelessly incapable of getting her sober, for all my new found wisdom.

"I cannot get my mother sober" I confided in a wise man one evening at an AA meeting. "I've tried everything" I said to him, "and it's not working." "Calm down Marilyn" the wise friend said. "Carry a message, not carry an alcoholic". "What do you mean" I queried. "She will see it works for you, and that will help her in return. Its called 'Power of

Example' so leave her be" he suggested, "and stop preaching to her." As I thanked my good friend for his wise advise, I only could pray she would get well and see this new 'Power of Example'.

Soon, it was to be sooner than I could ever have imagined when one month later on a very cold winters night in 1985, I was getting ready to go and speak at an AA meeting. On seeing my mother emerge from the bedroom, all cleaned up and ready to go out, with full make up, hair brushed and tidied up totally. I looked at her and genuinely asked "Are you going to the pub?" "No" she grunted, "I'm going to that meeting with you. I've a feeling you're talking about me at that place, and I'm going to see what it is all about." Good God, was I seeing and hearing right? Was my mother willingly going for help? Yes. Yes! Yes! Thank God that is truly the power of example and on that night, in the same year as myself, my mother got sober. Yes, yes, yes it works. God works. If you want him to work, and I love that.

This was unheard of, two hopeless cases sober? We were truly as mother and daughter two miracles. The two 'town drunks' sober, this was truly beyond my wildest dreams and I was on a total high with happiness. Me and my mother got sober, because we wanted it. We had to want sobriety so bad to get it, and we did. Call it the Power of Example, call it being reborn call it Gods intervention, call it whatever you like, all I could call it was two miracles in the one year. Two hopeless cases sober in the same year. Yes, it had to be a miracle, we could never have done it alone. God had to be involved for that one. Our lives started to get better and better, for it could not have got any worse, the simple fact that we were sober had to be better for us, and everyone around us.

I had found a good sales day job in an electrical store in town and I began to do so very well in my sales career. Sadly, there were two female sales assistants at the store whom resented me totally. Their resentment was really becoming an obsession with them. So much so, that when I would have a lunch break they would actually close the store and have a meeting of staff to discuss how to "get rid" of me. I would return from my lunch break and the shop would be closed with them around a staff table. Discussing me. They treated me like dirt, ignoring me in the shop, stealing my customers from me, telling my customers I was on my day off when I was actually upstairs in the stock room working on the premises all the time.

My life was unbearable at work but my job was delightful. I loved my sales position and I was top sales in the company every week in life. This angered the two sales women ever more, so much so, that on my day off, they stupidly summoned the Area Manager down to the shop to complain about my sales ability. "She is getting all the commission" they moaned to him. "We want a better slice of the commission cake, a fairer slice." He listened to this absurd request. According to what he later divulged to me, and then he said "Just what do you want me to do about Marilyn? The top sales person?" "We want you to stop her selling so much, so that we can all sell something". "We want her brought down to our sales level" they exclaimed. "What?" the area manager cried. "You either buck yourself up to her sales level or you both are out. Now, getting me here today to complain about a sales person selling too much, is just a complete piece of nonsense and a waste of my time. So get on with getting yourselves up to her sales level instead you fools" he continued.

On my return to work my Area Manager summoned me into his office to tell me of the resentments at the store, but I had already known about the major hatred problem in the shop. But thank God, I managed to rise above it with my teachings and help from my true friend, I was actually taught how to rise above it. You can only take a resentment, not be given one, and whilst I sleep peacefully the people who resent me, are walking the floor with hatred. So sad for them.

Time passed and my sobriety only strengthened. From day to day, even my bad days were great days because I was not drinking. I have always had the wisdom to know today, that as drink is not the answer to my problems, it very likely would be the cause of them and I would only see my problems multiply with drink. Four swift happy sober years had passed for my mother and myself, with my wonderful husband reaping the benefits of our new sober life.

I could see the major change for the better in my husband daily, with peace, trust, and contentment now a big part of his life now too. I was truly so so very happy until one day, I noticed my mother was becoming very pale and frail. She was also so happy with sobriety and actually still worked with her music career both she and I, were once more rising like Phoenix from the ashes with our music. I was returning to my beloved singing and my mother was still playing her accordion, with both of us now being wanted at major functions rather than shunned. Life was good and I loved that.

Still the niggling doubt annoyed me about my mother's weight loss. "I'm ok," she'd say, "I'm not going to a doctor with nothing wrong with me," she would insist. "Stop smoking" I would nag, nag, nag, "Indeed I will not" she exclaimed. "Didn't I do enough stopping drinking? I'm not giving up my only other pleasure" she'd cry, lighting up yet another one of her many roll-ups. She would chain smoke on a daily continual basis. She even had a roll-up machine which churned out ready made cigarettes on supply and demand, and my mother would line up all her ready made rolled up cigarettes like little soldiers all laid out ready to be smoked, and I'd swear she would eat them. They would disappear so fast.

"I've a dreadful pain in my back" she said quietly one day.

"I know what it is, I know I've pulled a muscle on my heavy accordion." "You must go to the doctor" I'd say. "Please please go to the doctor" I cried. "Oh alright" she squealed "but I know what's wrong, I've told you I've pulled a muscle. Perhaps it was even done by me pulling up my washing on the kitchen drying pulley." "Just go" I insisted "and get it fixed." Reluctantly, my mother headed for the doctors surgery the following day. With the doctor immediately sending her to the Glasgow Western Infirmary for various out patient tests. However, three weeks later whilst at my day job, I received a call from my mother's doctor, whom requested I call in that evening alone to discuss my mother's results.

As the doctor was a family friend, this was quite a usual request. "I can bring my mother in" I replied, "No Marilyn, I wish to discuss with you firstly." I froze with a sick fear at what my mother's results might be. I was truly frozen sick to the spot. "I'll come in now" I explained. As I put the phone down I was in such a state of shock, at what was facing me, I immediately got my coat and told my manager I'd have to go now to my mother's doctor. As I approached the surgery, my sick heart was sinking fast to my boots, and when the doctor welcomed me into the surgery I tried oh, my God, I tried to prepare myself for the worst. But I could not do this, for what the doctor was about to tell me could not have got any worse.

"The results of your mothers tests show a tumour on the lung and sadly it does not look good at all." "What do you mean?" I cried, "Can you operate?" "No Marilyn". "Sadly it would be malignant, the tumour has eaten through two ribs, it is sadly just too late." I began to scream, "No, no, no, don't tell me this, what are you saying?" "Are you saying Doctor, she will die?" "Yes sadly I'm sorry to say most definitely yes" he replied. "How long? How long are you talking about? A year?" I cried "Two years?" I cried. "No Marilyn" the doctor replied, "probably two months more like." Oh, no, no, no, dear God no. "The cancer is due to cigarette smoking and sadly this is the result." The doctor continued, as I continued to sob and sob in a hopeless despair, a truly hopeless despair.

As I headed home on the train that evening, I sat alone on the train. I sat alone in the corner of the carriage crying and crying with passengers all going about their usual business. Here was I in another world of my own sadness, shock, and true horror. How in under God was I going to accept this? How was I going to face my mother or look into her eyes knowing what I knew now? Oh God, they hadn't prepared me for this at my teachings, but they did, for I did not lift a drink, that would not have saved my mother nor helped me to cope, no I did not want a drink.

Cancer was never mentioned between my mother and myself at all, even after she obtained her results. She was still in denial maintaining she had pulled a muscle. The two months death sentence the doctor had given my mother were going fast, with my mother to and fro to hospital for radiotherapy, and her pain sadly becoming worse for her to bare. I shall never ever forget the day in particular when she and I were alone in the living room and her doctor called in to see her.

I sat on the big chair and my mother and doctor sat on the couch. As my mother continued to churn out her roll-up cigarettes from her machine, the doctor exclaimed; "Patricia, it's a smoke related illness you have". "Its cigarettes that's caused your cancer" and that very moment she physically threw the tobacco, papers, machine all from the coffee table in front of her, into the hearth of the fire, got onto her knees on the floor, pulled the doctors sleeves from his jacket and pleaded. She cried and pleaded "I'll give them up, I'll give them up now, please help me doctor" she cried. Well, at this moment I was so choked up with grief I had to remove myself from the room and as I stood crying in the hallway, on looking through the small crack in the doorway, I watched the doctor rise from his seat, gather up the smoking equipment from the hearth and place it all back into my poor mothers hands. "Smoke away Patricia, you're too late." My heart was broken. Truly broken. The prayers in the beginning of my mothers illness were all for a miracle "God save her, God keep her with me." But this changed radically when on the third month of my mother's cancer they admitted her to the local hospice. Tommy and I sat with her, only watching hopelessly the horrific deterioration in my mother and when I took a flu with a throat infection, the nuns and doctors forbade me from visiting the hospice for one week. Well, friends that week in my mothers life term was like a year to me. The week dragged on forever, and finally when I was allowed entry and visitation to the hospice, unknown to me, they had moved my mother's bed and I had actually walked past my own mother. I did not know her, she had deteriorated so very very much I actually had walked past her bed. I did not recognise my mother. That is my friends, when the prayers changed. "Take her now, my dear God, take her today. Don't let her suffer another day."

My mother's funeral was so very quiet and dignified, unlike my Granny's funeral. This time I was sober, she died sober too and I was able to bury her with dignity. Not this funeral would I be thrown from the chapel drunk. No, I did not want drink only four sober years together was don't forget, four sober years. More than we would ever have had, should we have continued to drink and I will treasure and remember those four sober years more than any others in my life. And I loved that.

Now 1990 I was now thirty six years old and made a conscious decision to find my father. I was five years old when he left and thirty one years had passed a whole life time. So he might not want to see me at all, I might not be able to find him at all. He could be in a new family now. He might deny me altogether or worse still with his chronic alcoholism he might be dead and buried. There was a barrage of ifs, and buts, and reasons for me not to find him but I had a strange determination to look for him at least if only to tell him of my mothers demise. Sure I had only just lost a parent, and it was so sad that I might have another one alive on this planet, and not know him. So I made my plan to find him. As I told my husband of my plans, he was so very supportive and agreed it was best for me to at least try to find him. But first, I must prepare myself for the worst rejection.

I had to harden myself totally as best I could for my father rejecting me, after all, he did do the same thing thirty one years ago. Although I never could bring myself to care or love him ever. I still felt so very orphaned now with my mother gone, so, I set my plans into action. Yes, should I have to get the Salvation Army, Red Cross, a private detective, or even Cilla Black on Surprise, Surprise to find him, by God I'd find him. I remembered I still had my aunt in Strabane Northern Ireland and my Aunt Ann was from my fathers side of the family and I vaguely remembered her from child hood. If I could get her phone number from directory enquiries it would be a start.

I dialled directory and started to explain my dilemma to the telephonist who was so very helpful and searched my aunt's name throughout the North of Ireland. For she had since moved residence and I had no clue of her address. At last we came on her name listed in the directory and I excitedly scribbled her number down and felt a bit of hope.

Tommy told me to go into the bedroom extension phone for more privacy, for he too is so thoughtful to my feelings and this I did. As I dialled my Aunt Ann's number I prayed to God it would lead me to my father. My Aunt Ann herself answered the phone, so very shocked to hear from me. We chatted about lots of things to begin with and I finally told her how my mother and I had got sober in the same year. My aunt was sad of my mother's death, but happy we got sober.

Then I dropped the clanger, "Do you know where my father is Aunt Ann?" There was a long silence, filled with what felt like hatred, anger and resentment for in the interim my father had "sold" businesses from under the family, for drink he had ran out on his own family and he was truly the black sheep of the family.

After a long pause, my aunt exclaimed "Him" "Do I know where he is?" "Do you know what he did to us here?" "Do you know how bad and awful he is?" and she proceeded to tell me a string of drunken horror he had performed. "He had to run out of the north of Ireland to Dublin that's all I know of him". "He could not even be contacted for his own mother's funeral, so don't mention his name to me" she fumed. "He's sleeping rough on the streets of Dublin and your better off without him". "Stay as you are Marilyn and be glad you've never found him." As I put the phone receiver down, I knew I must and would find him. So I came from the bedroom to my husband in the living room and Tommy said sympathetically "How did you get on?" "Ach, she doesn't want to know, even his name annoys her. But I'll find him, I know I'll find him."

Tommy put his arms around me to comfort me and reassured me once more not to "build up my hope". Half an hour passed when unexpectedly my telephone rang. As I lifted the receiver I realised it was my Aunt Ann once more on the line. "About your father, well as I said," she said dryly, "God knows where he is, but I've got a phone number of an old neighbour woman, of his. She is very old and I don't think she will know of his whereabouts. I don't even know if he or the neighbour woman are still even living at all." With that, I thanked her, scribbling the old woman's phone number down, I could feel a sense of excited hope rising within my heart.

So before I dialled the number I prepared myself for the worst rejection. When I pulled myself together enough, I dialled the Dublin phone number and eventually a very shaky old woman's voice answered "Hello" she croaked. "Hello" I said enthusiastically "I'm sorry to trouble you but I wonder does a Mr. ……," and I gave her my father's name, "Does he live near you?" "Oh yes" she said shakily "He lives in the old caravan across the street." Oh my God, I'd found him. "I'm his daughter" I exclaimed "and I've not seen him for thirty one years." There was a long pause then "Jesus, Mary and Joseph" came flowing out of the old woman's lips amongst various other saints names. "You're his daughter?" she squeaked very frail in voice. "Yes" I said, "Could you run across the street and get him for me?" I shrieked. Run, could she run? Dear God she could barely stand up never mind run. "Yes, yes" she replied. "Phone back in ten minutes and I'll fetch him."

The time dragged, and as I walked the floor with my husband by my side, a horrific thought crossed my mind. "Oh my God forgive me Tommy" I said, "What if the old neighbour woman collapses in the street and I never find my Dad?" "Oh, shut up Marilyn, don't talk stupid." Tommy's faith in God was slightly stronger than mine at that point. As I nervously dialled the number once more, my father answered "Hello" I said nervously, "Its Marilyn" I continued. As I waited for him to perhaps reject me or whatever, he then said "I'm astonished". "I cannot believe you've found me! Thirty one years a whole lifetime gone and you've found me." I gibbered and chatted nervously like a budgie all my news. "My mother died" I cried, "We got sober together" I cried. I continued to twitter on and on mainly with nerves. "Christmas is in two weeks. I shall come over and see you for Christmas" my father said. Oh, God I'm going to meet him as soon. Two weeks time. As I hung up the phone, I clung and cried to my husband "I've found him, I've found him. I've found him at last Tommy!" Tommy was so happy for me and as I got ready to go to my AA meeting I actually felt like a five year old child who had just found her father. I was actually back to the age I was when he left. "I've found my father" I was squealing to my friends who were so happy for me too.

As I got home that night there was a telephone message on my machine from the old neighbour women in Dublin. "This is just to say" she croaked, "Your father will be on the nine o'clock flight to Glasgow in the morning" and she hung up. The morning? The morning? I was going to meet him tomorrow, not two weeks away tomorrow morning. Oh my God, not even twenty four hours away I found him at last.

Our reunion was beautiful at Glasgow airport. Although he was now sixty three years old and battered with his poor lifestyle, I knew him. I knew him right away. "There he is" I said to Tommy. And not only was the shock of finding him unbelievable, but what he said next nearly floored me. Through hugs and tears he said to me "I got sober Marilyn in 1985." "What?" the same year as me and my mother, I could not believe my ears, 1985. Mother, father, and daughter, we all three got sober in the same year.

I had to sit down, for fear of fainting on hearing the strange coincidence. It was a very unreal feeling. Fair enough, thank God we all got sober, but in the same year, was uncanny. Meeting my father was a wonderful new chapter in my new life. He would nor could never replace my mother, but he was my father and the finding of him helped me so much to get over my mothers recent death. We would sit up all night long, him and I chatting about the past. His wild lifestyle, for he had truly lost so much. He never had any more children, I joked "One look at me and he ran, that was enough". "No" he said, "I had lost enough my wife, my daughter family and businesses," every possession he owned he lost through alcoholism. He slept on park benches, streets etc, another no –hoper. Until 1985, he got sober.

There truly are no hopeless cases. My father and I have come a long long way since finding each other. I had a bit of forgiving to do and forgetting his past too. I know I could not carry resentment or anger into the present day, or there would be no future. I've accepted he did wrong doings, so did I. In alcoholism, the illness we both suffer from, helps us to forgive for the past, as clinging onto empty regrets its no use to anyone. What we have done is get on with what we have now.

My father, since our reunion, only one year later suffered a stroke. I was with him when he took ill and my panic was beyond belief. After having only known and found him one year, I was now so very afraid that I was about to lose him. But, with the grace of God, and much determination from my father, he thankfully recovered, and has lived on, to enjoy a happy sober life today. My husband and I, have since moved to my beloved Ireland, and see my father regularly.

My life today is so very wonderful in comparison to my drunken days. I have continued with my music, and have been very fortunate to perform alongside some very famous Irish musicians indeed. Although I have a few bouts of illness myself, in my sober years, I am today thank God, very well. I also know the difference today that my health is my wealth. My husband, my father, and myself have now a life truly beyond our wildest dreams. Remember friends, there are no such things as "Hopeless Cases." If sobriety can turn my beloved mother, my father, and especially my own hopeless life around that alone, is total proof to strive for a dream and you will get there, a sober dream in my case.

The beauty of life today for my father and I, is the very fact that we do not want drink. That is how beautiful our life and sobriety is today. Why in under God would we give that all away for a lousy drink? We have been gifted. I can just hear my beloved Mother and Granny looking down on us three, and chuckle, "Look mother, Marilyn's got those two just as tortured as she used to torture us" and my Granny good naturedly replying "Aye, Tricia, but at least today it's a sober torture", "For I could never have rested in peace, seeing my whole family destroyed with alcohol." And Reader, I firmly believe with my Granny's strong faith, and direct line to the Lord, she definitely had a big hand in our sobriety. My father and I are now twenty years sober, more years sober, than I drank but also twenty years older, and although this is pure magic, I have to laugh also, when my father cheerily comments "Marilyn, twenty years sober is truly a wonderful miracle!" "But, we also have to take the grey hair, false teeth and wrinkles that go along with it." I laugh at him, and his quirky sense of humour, but I never forgot, that my sobriety is a very serious programme, and I love and treasure it with a total passion. That is some passion Reader, for don't forget, with me, there is 'No Half Measures'. And I love that.

Marilyn

1) **No Matter What**
Andrew Lloyd Webber/ Jim Steinman Really Useful Group (PUB)

2) **Little Arrows**
A. Hmmond B.M.I.

3) **Crazy**
Willie Nelson Acuff Rose Music

4) **Salt In My Tears**
Dolly Parton Velvet Apple Music B.M.I.

5) **Make Me An Island**
Hammond/ Hazelwood Lou Vigny Publishing

6) **Things**
Bobby Darren B.M.I.

7) **Over and Over (Again)**
D. Gray/ P.Renleau W. Chaln NID Pub. Co.

8) **Blanket On The Ground**
R. Bowling Campbell Connelly Music

9) **I Just Want To Dance With You**
J. Prine/ R. Cook Big Ears Music & Bruised Orange

10) **It's You, It's You, It's You.**
R. Donova Quartermass Music

11) **Love You Every Second**
C. Lansburgh Ace Music Pub. Ltd

12) **Your One And Only**
E. Stephens/ H. Kanter E.S.P. Music B.M.I.

Special Thanks to
Clive Cullbertson - Piano/ Backing Vocals Joe Mcnamee - Guitar/ Pedal Steel
John Currie - Photograhy Ballymoney

Engineering & Production Clive Cullbertson
No Sweat Studios Colerine
Re-mixed at C.P.R. Studios. Bangor by Austen Lennon
Additional Gultars - Chris Blair